THE LIST

A MODERN GUIDE TO DATING

Kennet Bath

authorHOUSE

AuthorHouse™ UK
1663 Liberty Drive
Bloomington, IN 47403 USA
www.authorhouse.co.uk
Phone: UK TFN: 0800 0148641 (Toll Free inside the UK)
        UK Local: (02) 0369 56322 (+44 20 3695 6322 from outside the UK)

Published by AuthorHouse 06/29/2023

ISBN: 979-8-8230-8347-8 (sc)
ISBN: 979-8-8230-8348-5 (e)

Library of Congress Control Number: 2023912120

Print information available on the last page.

This book is printed on acid-free paper.

AUTHOR'S NOTE

Welcome to THE LIST: A Modern Guide to Dating.

This book explores the complexities of modern dating, offering insights and practical strategies for finding love in today's fast-paced world. Whether you're single and looking for companionship or seeking to strengthen your existing relationship, this book provides advice to navigate the dating landscape and build meaningful connections.

The idea for this book originated from a conversation I had with a friend after our marriages ended. We reflected on our failed relationships and wondered what led us to choose our partners in the first place. We realized that certain criteria played a role, such as shared interests and physical attraction. However, we also acknowledged that relying solely on a checklist was unrealistic and could lead to relationship failure.

Thus, "The List" was born - a set of criteria outlining the qualities and interests we desire in a partner. We indulged in our fantasies and created extensive lists, but we soon realized the impossibility of finding someone who embodies all those qualities. We understood that perfection doesn't exist, not even within ourselves.

This book is the result of our discussions and reflections. It aims to provide tools and insights for the world of dating. While no one is perfect, certain aspects may be more important than others when seeking a compatible partner. Enjoy the journey!

Kennet Bath
June 2023

CONTENTS

Conclusion: "The List: A Modern Guide to Dating and Relationships" provides a roadmap for individuals seeking genuine connections in a world saturated with fleeting encounters. It emphasizes the importance of self-discovery, effective communication, and emotional intelligence while providing practical tools to overcome challenges and nurture healthy relationships. Remember, love is a journey, and by investing in your-self and fostering authentic connections, you can create a fulfilling and meaningful ro-mantic life. Happy dating!

CHAPTER 1

UNDERSTANDING YOURSELF
AND WHAT YOU WANT

CHAPTER 1 - Understanding Yourself and what you want

Think about what do you want?

Have you ever taken the time to consider what you truly desire? It may seem like a peculiar question, but it's a commonly accepted notion that many individuals are unaware of their deepest aspirations and interests until they delve into self-reflection. Discovering what you truly want in life requires asking yourself thought-provoking questions: How do you envision your ideal existence? What brings you genuine joy and fulfillment? What holds the utmost significance to you? In the following pages, we will provide you with invaluable tools to facilitate this journey of self-discovery and help you establish a clear understanding of your own identity. Additionally, we will guide you in defining the qualities and characteristics you desire in a potential partner. However, it is crucial to acknowledge that unraveling your own desires and aspirations is the fundamental task at hand.

Before embarking on a dating journey, it's crucial to ask yourself, "What are your desires and goals?" Without a clear understanding of what you want, it becomes challenging to attain those desires. So, how can you go about discovering your true desires? In my opinion, it all begins with daring to dream.

I remember telling my children when they were young, "You can be anything you want. Dare to dream, because without dreams, you have nothing." Whether they aspired to be rock stars, actors, or even warehouse workers, I encouraged them to pursue their passions. The same principle applies to your choice of a life partner. Opt for a firsthand choice, betting on what you genuinely want, rather than settling for a secondhand option.

When considering what you desire in a future partner, don't restrict yourself from the start. Embrace the possibilities and allow yourself to explore different avenues. Maybe your ideal partner shares your love for running marathons, appreciates sport cars, or embodies qualities like Beyoncé. The key is to begin grading your preferences, acknowledging that certain aspects hold more significance than others.

During a conversation with my friend, we tried to avoid superficial desires while prioritizing our shared interests. Although physical attractiveness may initially seem important, in the long run, it holds little significance. Instead, we emphasized the importance of shared interests. For instance, imagine being passionate about golf and having the opportunity to play regularly, but your partner has no interest in the sport. It becomes evident that sacrifices may be necessary depending on the extent of your passion. I have a friend who is immensely passionate about 1950s cars. Besides work, his life revolves around these vehicles, spending every spare minute in the garage. It's safe to say that having a partner who shares his enthusiasm for cars would greatly enhance his happiness. Therefore, similar interests play a substantial role in fostering a fulfilling relationship.

Once you have identified what you want, it's crucial to pursue it without making excessive compromises. The more your potential partner deviates from your desires, the more compromises and strain your relationship may endure. Many individuals spend their entire lives with partners who have vastly different interests. Rarely does anything on their lists align with their partner's attributes. While this is a valid way to live, it's essential to ask yourself: does this path lead to genuine happiness? From my perspective, it does not. However, it's not my place to judge, as everyone lives the life they desire.

Understanding your desires requires prioritization of your goals and aspirations, be it in relationships, careers, or other aspects of life. Having a clear sense of your wants and needs serves as a solid foundation for decision-making and the pursuit of happiness.

In the realm of relationships, comprehending what you want entails a deep understanding of your own values, interests, and aspirations. It means recognizing the qualities and attributes that hold importance to you in a partner and envisioning the type of relationship that aligns with your aspirations. This self-awareness empowers you to make conscious choices that harmonize with your long-term objectives and personal fulfillment.

While compromise is an inherent aspect of any relationship, it's vital not to settle for less or compromise excessively. Finding a balance between flexibility and staying true to your values and aspirations is key. While differences can bring diversity and enrichment to a relationship, significant disparities in values, interests, and goals may lead to constant compromises and disagreements. Over time, this can erode the relationship and impede personal growth and happiness.

Living a life where your partner does not share your interests and values may be a conscious choice for some individuals. However, it's essential to reflect on whether such a life genuinely brings happiness and fulfillment. Although it's not for anyone to judge how others choose to live

Here's a sample version of my own list:

1. Share a Christian faith.
2. Have similar sexual preferences.
3. Appreciate physical affection.
4. Value fitness and enjoy maintaining a healthy lifestyle.
5. Prioritize spending quality time together.
6. Have a passion for traveling.
7. Desire to live in two different countries.
8. Have adult children.
9. Share the same values when it comes to raising children.
10. Share similar ethics and morals.
11. Prefer remote work opportunities.
12. Possess an entrepreneurial mindset.
13. Maintain good personal hygiene and smell pleasant.
14. Practice proper table manners, such as not eating with an open mouth.

These are the answers I sought during my interview with her. I wonder how many items on my list align with her thoughts. Additionally, I'm curious to know if she has any significant concerns or obstacles that could potentially hinder our collaboration. It is important to carefully consider your own desires and objectives when compiling your own list.

Is the list ever constant? Not really. It undergoes continual transformation influenced by age and experience, presenting an element of uncertainty. Even if you believe you've found a "perfect match," personal growth can lead you in divergent paths over time. It's widely acknowledged that age significantly impacts this process. As you progress through life, your self-awareness and preferences become more defined. The list, as I perceive it, is an organic entity in a perpetual state of flux. However, by prioritizing the most significant aspects, you still have a wonderful opportunity to evolve together.

Now, let's embark on our journey. I've compiled the majority of the book's content as a list. Why did I choose this format? I believe it makes the recommendations more accessible and straightforward for you to peruse. I trust that you share the same sentiment and find it easier to navigate through the list. And yeah... The name of the book is THE LIST.

Discovering your values, passions, and goals
So, what do you want? Discovering your values, passions, and goals is a transformative journey that allows you to gain a deeper understanding of yourself and live a more fulfilling life. It involves exploring your core beliefs, uncovering your true desires, and setting meaningful objectives that align with who you are at your core. By engaging in this process, you can pave the way for personal growth, happiness, and a sense of purpose.

Values serve as the guiding principles that shape your decisions, actions, and behaviors. They are the fundamental beliefs that reflect what you consider important in life. Discovering your values involves reflecting on what truly matters to you and identifying the principles that you want to live by. It requires self-exploration and introspection, as well as considering the aspects of life that bring you the greatest sense of fulfillment and contentment. By recognizing your values, you can make choices that are in alignment with your authentic self and lead a life that feels meaningful and purposeful.

Passions are the activities, interests, or pursuits that ignite a fire within you. They are the things that you are naturally drawn to and derive great joy, enthusiasm, and satisfaction from. Discovering your passions involves exploring various areas of interest, trying new experiences, and paying attention to the activities that make you lose track of time or evoke a sense of flow. By tapping into your passions, you can infuse your life with energy and excitement, and engage in activities that bring you a deep sense of fulfillment and happiness.

Goals are the desired outcomes or achievements that you strive for in various areas of your life. They provide a sense of direction and purpose, giving you something to work towards and motivating you to take action. Discovering your goals involves envisioning the future you desire, both in the short term and the long term. It requires clarifying what you want to accomplish and identifying the steps necessary to reach those milestones. By setting goals that are aligned with your values and passions, you can create a roadmap for personal and professional growth and experience a sense of fulfillment as you make progress towards your aspirations.

To embark on the journey of discovering your values, passions, and goals, consider the following steps:

1. **Self-reflection:** Set aside time for introspection and self-exploration. Ask yourself meaningful questions about what truly matters to you, what activities bring you joy, and what kind of future you envision for yourself.

2. **Experimentation:** Try new experiences and engage in activities that pique your curiosity. Explore different hobbies,

interests, and areas of knowledge. Pay attention to what resonates with you and brings you a sense of fulfillment.

3. **Mindfulness:** Practice mindfulness and be fully present in your daily life. Pay attention to the moments that evoke positive emotions and take note of the activities that make you feel alive and engaged.

4. **Personal values assessment:** Take a values assessment or engage in exercises designed to help you identify your core values. Reflect on the principles and beliefs that are most important to you and shape your decisions.

5. **Goal setting:** Reflect on your values and passions and use them as a foundation for setting meaningful goals. Break your goals down into actionable steps and create a plan to work towards them.

6. **Adaptation and growth:** Understand that your values, passions, and goals may evolve over time. Be open to reevaluating and adapting them as you gain new insights and experiences.

Discovering your values, passions, and goals is a lifelong journey. It requires self-awareness, self-compassion, and a willingness to explore different aspects of yourself. Embrace the process with an open mind and heart and be patient with yourself as you uncover what truly matters to you. By aligning your life with your authentic self, you can create a meaningful and fulfilling existence that reflects your deepest desires and aspirations.

CHAPTER 2

ONLINE DATING AND APPS

CHAPTER 2 – Online dating and Apps

Navigating the world of online dating and choosing the right platform

Navigating the world of online dating can be both exciting and overwhelming. With numerous platforms available, each offering its own unique features and user base, it's essential to choose the right platform that aligns with your dating goals and preferences. Whether you're looking for a serious relationship, casual dating, or simply expanding your social circle, understanding the key factors to consider will help you make an informed decision.

1. **Define your dating goals:** Before selecting an online dating platform, take some time to reflect on what you're seeking in a relationship. Are you looking for a long-term commitment, companionship, or a casual fling? Knowing your objectives will guide your choice of platform and help you filter out options that don't align with your desires.

2. **Research different platforms:** Familiarize yourself with the various online dating platforms available. Popular platforms like Tinder, Bumble, OkCupid, Match.com, and eHarmony cater to different audiences and dating preferences. Read reviews, compare features, and consider the platform's reputation for successful matches in your area. Look for platforms with a significant user base to increase your chances of finding compatible matches.

3. **Consider the demographic and target audience:** Different dating platforms attract different demographics. Some cater to specific age groups, religious affiliations, or sexual orientations. Research the platform's user base to ensure it aligns with your preferences. This will enhance your chances of connecting with like-minded individuals who share your values and interests.

4. **Evaluate the platform's features:** Each dating platform offers a range of features to enhance your experience. Some focus on swiping and quick matches, while others emphasize detailed profiles and compatibility algorithms. Consider which features are important to you. For instance, if you value in-depth profiles and compatibility matching, platforms like eHarmony or Match.com might be suitable. If you prefer a more casual and interactive approach, Tinder or Bumble might be worth exploring.

5. **Safety and privacy measures:** Online safety is paramount when engaging in online dating. Research the platform's safety measures, such as profile verification, reporting and blocking options, and encryption of personal data. Ensure that the platform prioritizes user safety and has robust policies in place to protect your information.

6. **Free vs. paid platforms:** Decide whether you're willing to invest in a paid dating platform or prefer to start with free options. Paid platforms often provide additional features, such as advanced search filters, message prioritization, and ad-free experiences. However, free platforms can still offer valuable connections, especially if you're new to online dating.

7. **Test the platform:** Once you've narrowed down your options, consider trying out multiple platforms simultaneously or sequentially. This will give you firsthand experience and help you gauge the platform's user interface, ease of use, and overall quality. Experimenting with different platforms will also allow you to explore different user bases and increase your chances of finding compatible matches.

8. **Adapt and refine:** Online dating is a dynamic process, and it's important to adapt and refine your approach as you gain experience. Be open to trying new platforms if your initial choice doesn't yield the desired results. Regularly update

your profile, review your search criteria, and engage actively with potential matches to maximize your chances of success.

Remember, finding the right online dating platform is just the first step. Building meaningful connections requires active participation, genuine communication, and a positive mindset. Stay patient, be yourself, and enjoy the journey of discovering new people and potential relationships in the digital dating landscape.

Crafting an attractive and authentic dating profile
Crafting an attractive and authentic dating profile is essential when it comes to online dating. Your profile serves as your introduction to potential matches, and it's crucial to make a positive and memorable impression. Here are some tips to help you create a profile that stands out and accurately represents who you are:

1. **Be honest and genuine:** Authenticity is key in online dating. Be true to yourself and portray your personality accurately. Don't try to be someone you're not or exaggerate your qualities. Highlight your genuine interests, hobbies, and values to attract like-minded individuals.

2. **Choose the right photos:** Your profile photos are the first thing potential matches will see, so it's important to select them carefully. Use high-quality pictures that clearly show your face and accurately represent your appearance. Include a mix of candid shots and pictures that reflect your interests and lifestyle. Please, never use filter on your photo! They will meet you in real life and see you true face, let it not be a negative surprise!

3. **Write a compelling bio:** Your bio is an opportunity to showcase your personality and give potential matches an insight into who you are. Keep it concise and engaging. Mention your hobbies, passions, and what you're looking for in a relationship. Use humor or unique anecdotes to grab attention and spark curiosity.

4. **Showcase your interests:** Talk about the things you love to do and the activities that bring you joy. Whether it's hiking, playing a musical instrument, or cooking, sharing your passions will attract people who share similar interests.

5. **Be positive and upbeat:** A positive attitude is attractive, so focus on showcasing your optimism and enthusiasm for life. Avoid mentioning past negative experiences or using negative language. Instead, highlight the things that make you happy and the qualities you appreciate in others. To talk much about your ex is normally no success.

6. **Be specific:** Vague statements can be uninspiring and make it difficult for others to connect with you. Instead, be specific about your interests and preferences. For example, instead of saying "I enjoy traveling," you could say "I love exploring new countries and immersing myself in different cultures."

7. **Show your sense of humor:** Humor is a fantastic way to grab attention and make a lasting impression. If you're naturally funny, don't be afraid to showcase it in your profile. A well-placed joke or witty comment can make you stand out from the crowd.

8. **Avoid clichés:** Phrases like "I love long walks on the beach" or "I'm looking for my soulmate" have become overused and can make your profile seem generic. Try to be more specific and original in describing yourself and what you're looking for. At the same time be honest. If you are looking for a partner for life, say that too. I've found out it is good to have the strength to be vulnerable.

9. **Proofread and edit:** Typos and grammar mistakes can create a negative impression, so take the time to proofread your profile before publishing it. A well-written and error-free profile demonstrates your attention to detail and shows that you've put effort into creating it.

10. **Be open-minded:** While it's good to have preferences and deal-breakers, it's important to remain open-minded when it comes to potential matches. Avoid setting rigid criteria and allow room for surprises. You might find a genuine connection with someone who doesn't fit your initial expectations or your list.

Remember, creating an attractive and authentic dating profile is just the first step. Be proactive in reaching out to potential matches, engage in meaningful conversations, and always be yourself. Good luck!

Effective strategies for connecting with potential matches
When it comes to connecting with potential matches, whether in the context of dating or professional networking, employing effective strategies can significantly increase your chances of establishing meaningful connections. Here are some strategies to consider:

1. **Be Authentic:** Authenticity is key when trying to connect with potential matches. Be genuine and true to yourself, as people are generally attracted to authenticity. Avoid presenting a false version of yourself or pretending to be someone you're not. Instead, focus on showcasing your unique qualities and interests. When I date, I choose to put forth every negative aspect of my personality, not holding back anything. In a world where people often put on masks to hide their imperfection, I want to break that pattern and show that it's okay to be flawed. In the long run I can't hide it anyway. By that I normally can surprise in a positive way.

2. **Active Listening:** Engage in active listening to show genuine interest in the other person. Ask open-ended questions and listen attentively to their responses. By actively listening, you demonstrate that you value their thoughts and opinions, fostering a deeper connection and understanding.

3. **Find Common Ground:** Look for common interests or shared experiences that you can discuss. Finding common ground provides a foundation for building a connection and encourages conversation to flow more naturally. It can be anything from hobbies, favorite books, or similar career paths.

4. **Show Empathy:** Demonstrating empathy is crucial in establishing connections. Try to understand and relate to the other person's experiences, emotions, and perspectives. Show empathy by acknowledging their feelings and offering support or encouragement when appropriate.

5. **Positive Body Language:** Non-verbal cues play a significant role in connecting with others. Maintain good eye contact, use open and welcoming body language, and smile genuinely. Positive body language conveys friendliness and approachability, making it easier for potential matches to feel comfortable around you.

6. **Be Respectful and Polite:** Treat others with respect and kindness. Be mindful of your tone and language, ensuring that you communicate in a polite and considerate manner. Respectful behavior creates a positive impression and fosters a conducive environment for meaningful connections.

7. **Find Common Goals:** If you are seeking a long-term relationship or a professional partnership, aligning your goals with the other person's goals can be essential. Discuss your aspirations, values, and future plans to identify if you share compatible visions. This alignment increases the likelihood of a strong connection.

8. **Share Vulnerabilities:** Sharing vulnerabilities can help build trust and intimacy in relationships. Opening up about your fears, challenges, or personal experiences can create a deeper connection and encourage the other person to reciprocate.

However, ensure you share vulnerabilities at an appropriate time and with people you trust.

9. **Follow Up and Stay Engaged:** After the initial interaction, it's important to stay engaged and follow up. Show your genuine interest and commitment to nurturing the connection by sending a thoughtful message, extending an invitation for a coffee or a virtual meeting, or continuing the conversation in a relevant manner. Avoid playing games and pretending to be uninterested if you genuinely have an interest in the person. Consistently staying engaged demonstrates your sincerity and strengthens the connection.

10. **Practice Patience:** Building connections takes time and effort. Don't rush the process or get discouraged if things don't progress quickly. Patience is key, as genuine connections often develop gradually. Keep an open mind and enjoy the journey of getting to know someone new.

Remember, everyone is unique, and not every connection will result in a match. However, by employing these strategies, you enhance your ability to connect with potential matches and increase the likelihood of establishing meaningful and fulfilling relationships.

Don't repeat your mistakes
Not making your mistakes twice is a secret in all areas of life. Easy right? Not at all, I would say. It requires a brave person to dare to look at himself with critical eyes.

"Don't repeat your mistakes" is a powerful mantra that emphasizes the importance of learning from our past experiences and avoiding the same errors in the future. It serves as a reminder to approach life with a sense of self-awareness and a willingness to grow and improve.

Recognizing and acknowledging our mistakes can be challenging. It requires us to set aside our ego and take a honest look at ourselves.

Often, we tend to rationalize or deny our errors, which hinders our personal and professional development. However, embracing our mistakes and understanding their causes and consequences is essential for growth.

When we make a mistake, it's crucial to analyze the situation objectively. We can ask ourselves questions such as: What went wrong? Why did it happen? How could I have handled it differently? By reflecting on these aspects, we gain valuable insights and lessons that help us avoid repeating the same mistakes in the future.

Learning from mistakes also involves taking responsibility for our actions. Instead of blaming external factors or other people, we acknowledge our role in the situation and understand that we have the power to make better choices. This accountability empowers us to make conscious decisions and implement positive changes.

Moreover, the process of not repeating mistakes requires ongoing self-reflection and continuous learning. It's not a one-time event, but rather a lifelong journey of personal growth. By cultivating a mindset of curiosity and openness, we become receptive to new perspectives and ideas. This allows us to adapt, evolve, and avoid falling into the same pitfalls.

In various areas of life, such as relationships, career, and personal development, the principle of not repeating mistakes remains relevant. In relationships, for example, it encourages effective communication, empathy, and understanding. By learning from past miscommunications or conflicts, we can foster healthier and more fulfilling connections.

Professionally, the mantra of not repeating mistakes promotes a culture of innovation and continuous improvement. Organizations that encourage their employees to learn from failures create an environment where creativity thrives, and new solutions emerge.

In summary, not repeating mistakes requires courage, self-reflection, and a commitment to personal growth. It is an ongoing process that involves learning from our past experiences, taking responsibility for our actions, and actively seeking improvement. By embracing this mindset, we can navigate life's challenges more effectively, make better decisions, and ultimately create a brighter future for ourselves.

In my company, which is an advertising agency, we measure all results. Every customer campaign we do is measured and analyzed for what went badly and well, respectively. When the next campaign is to be made, we take into account previous results and eliminate what previously went badly. At every step we refine and improve. After hundreds of jobs, the results have been really good. Why? We don't make our mistakes twice. In this way, you should also look at your relationship. Now, many of us don't have hundreds of relationships behind us, so we have to learn on a smaller scale and not with the same precision as in the advertising agency.

Analyzing your past life as you lived is the start. If you've had a long relationship before that ended, there was a reason, I promise. When I ended my previous marriage, there was of course a period of not understanding anything. How could things go the way they did, me who is such a wonderful person to live with, maybe even the most wonderful person on earth. How did it end? Simple, it was all the partner's fault! If she hadn't fussed so much, been a little more "accommodating" and considerate, then everything would have been fine. But with some time and distance, I began to look at my part of the relationship. Was I as amazing as my self-image seems to be?

Unfortunately, or maybe luckily, I could state that my effort might not have been so brilliant. Many small things I could have done much better, and some things were disasters. What I could tell was that it should clearly be showstoppers in any potential partner. It was horrible to realize that I was no better than this and that I was responsible for most of the shortcomings. I don't want to make these mistakes again! It is far too high a price to pay for a failed marriage to repeat the same mistake. Someone once said that the height of stupidity is to repeat today the same mistake I made yesterday but expect a different result! There is something in it. What I've done is to see my mistakes and try to correct them (now I certainly haven't seen all my flaws, but it's a good first step). This process, I know today after two failed marriages, is for me a constant looking in the mirror to refine and correct. But I want to be the best version of myself, do you want that?

So, we quickly repeat, analyzing and ignoring past mistakes will save yourself a lot of negative experiences. But it is important to first dare to find out your shortcomings for yourself. Easy huh? :-)

CHAPTER 3

UDERSTANDING FAKE PROFILES

Chapter 3 – Understanding fake profiles

Fake profiles
Welcome to the murky realm of online dating, where the virtual landscape is teeming with opportunities to meet new people and potentially find love. However, amidst the vast array of genuine' profiles, there lurks a shadowy presence - fake profiles and scams. In this chapter, we will explore the deceptive world of fake profiles, uncover common scams, and equip you with valuable insights and techniques to avoid falling victim to these online traps.

Navigating the treacherous waters of online dating requires awareness, vigilance, and a healthy dose of skepticism. Fake profiles and scams may attempt to deceive and exploit but armed with the knowledge and techniques outlined in this chapter, you can protect yourself from falling victim to these digital charlatans. Remember, your safety and happiness are paramount, so trust your instincts, conduct thorough research, and establish authentic connections with genuine individuals who truly deserve your time and affection.

Understanding fake profiles
Understanding fake profiles when dating is important to protect yourself from potential scams or deceptive behavior. Fake profiles can be created by individuals with malicious intentions, such as catfishing, identity theft, or financial fraud. Here are some tips to help you identify and deal with fake profiles:

1. **Inconsistent or overly attractive photos:** Fake profiles often use pictures of attractive individuals, sometimes even celebrities or stock photos. If the person's photos seem too perfect or if their appearance seems too good to be true, it could be a warning sign.

2. **Limited or vague information:** Fake profiles typically provide limited or vague information about the person. They may not have detailed descriptions about themselves,

their interests, or their background. This lack of personal information is a red flag.

3. **Poor grammar and spelling:** Many fake profiles are created by scammers who may not be native English speakers or use automated translation tools. As a result, their messages may contain noticeable grammar and spelling mistakes. Pay attention to these errors as they can indicate a fake profile.

4. **Immediate request for personal information or money:** Be cautious if someone you just met online asks for personal information, financial assistance, or tries to rush you into sharing personal details. Legitimate individuals will take their time getting to know you before asking for sensitive information or financial support.

5. **Inconsistent or contradictory stories:** Pay attention to inconsistencies in the information they share. Fake profiles may have stories that don't align or change over time. If something doesn't add up or if their stories seem too perfect, it's a cause for concern.

6. **Lack of availability for video calls or in-person meetings:** Fake profiles often avoid video calls or meeting in person. They may come up with excuses or claim they don't have access to video chat services. This behavior is a warning sign that the person may not be who they claim to be.

7. **Reverse image search:** If you're suspicious about someone's profile pictures, you can perform a reverse image search. Use search engines like Google or specialized tools to see if the images are found elsewhere online. If the images appear on multiple websites or belong to someone else, it's likely a fake profile.

Remember, it's important to trust your instincts. If something feels off or too good to be true, it's wise to proceed with caution or end the interaction altogether. Always prioritize your safety and be vigilant when engaging with others online.

Motivations Behind Creating Fake Profiles
Creating fake profiles on dating platforms can stem from various motivations, some of which are driven by genuine intentions, while others are rooted in deceitful or malicious purposes. Understanding the motivations behind the creation of fake dating profiles requires considering a range of factors and individual circumstances. Here are a few common motivations that might lead someone to create a fake profile when dating:

1. **Experimentation or Curiosity:** Some individuals may create fake profiles out of curiosity or a desire to explore different personas. They may be interested in observing how people respond to certain characteristics or behaviors. This motivation is often driven by a sense of adventure or a desire to gain insights into human interaction.

2. **Entertainment or Pranks:** Certain individuals may create fake profiles for amusement or to play pranks on others. They may find pleasure in deceiving or misleading unsuspecting users, using fabricated identities to engage with them. While this motivation is largely lighthearted, it can still lead to confusion, frustration, and emotional distress for those who fall victim to the ruse.

3. **Emotional Validation:** Some individuals may feel a need for attention, validation, or emotional support that they are unable to receive in their own lives. By creating a fake profile, they can assume a persona that they believe will attract the attention and validation they crave. This motivation is often driven by a longing for connection and affirmation.

4. **Financial Exploitation:** Unfortunately, dating platforms can attract individuals seeking financial gain through fraudulent means. They may create fake profiles with the intention of

scamming others, using emotional manipulation to extract money or personal information. These scammers often prey on vulnerable individuals who may be seeking love or companionship.

5. **Catfishing or Deception:** Catfishing refers to the act of creating a fake profile to establish a romantic or emotional relationship with someone under false pretenses. Motivations for catfishing can vary widely, including seeking revenge, experiencing the thrill of deception, or compensating for personal insecurities. In some cases, catfishers may also exploit their victims emotionally, psychologically, or financially.

It is important to note that creating fake profiles for fraudulent or malicious purposes is unethical and can cause harm to unsuspecting individuals. It violates the trust and integrity of online dating platforms, negatively impacting genuine users seeking authentic connections.

Dating platforms continuously work towards implementing measures to detect and prevent the creation of fake profiles, such as employing identity verification processes, AI algorithms, and user reporting systems. Users are encouraged to remain vigilant, exercise caution, and report any suspicious or fraudulent activity they encounter to ensure a safer and more trustworthy dating environment.

Catfishing
Catfishing refers to the act of creating a fake online persona to deceive and manipulate others, typically for personal gain, emotional manipulation, or even malicious intent. The term "catfish" originated from a documentary called "Catfish," which explored a complex online relationship built on false identities. Since then, catfishing has become a prevalent issue in the digital age, affecting individuals across various social media platforms, dating websites, and online communities.

The motivations behind catfishing can vary. Some people engage in catfishing for personal validation or to escape their own realities. They may create elaborate stories and fabricate details about their lives, appearance, and backgrounds to appear more appealing or sympathetic to their targets. This deception can lure unsuspecting individuals into emotionally invested relationships, which can have devastating consequences when the truth is eventually revealed.

In other cases, catfishing may involve financial exploitation. The catfish may convince their targets to send money, gifts, or personal information under false pretenses. They may manipulate their victims' emotions, exploiting their vulnerabilities and trust to gain access to their financial resources.

Catfishing can also have severe emotional repercussions. Victims often experience feelings of betrayal, humiliation, and confusion when they discover they have been deceived. The impact on their self-esteem and ability to trust others can be long-lasting, leading to emotional trauma and difficulties in future relationships.

To avoid falling victim to catfishing, it is essential to be vigilant and exercise caution while interacting with others online. Here are some precautions you can take:

1. **Verify identities:** If you suspect someone may be catfishing you, try to confirm their identity through various means, such as video calls or asking for pictures in real-time situations. Be wary of individuals who consistently refuse or make excuses to avoid such verification.

2. **Be cautious with personal information:** Avoid sharing sensitive personal information with individuals you have only met online. This includes financial details, home addresses, or any other information that could be used against you.

3. **Trust your instincts:** If something feels off or too good to be true, trust your gut instincts. If someone seems overly

perfect or makes unrealistic promises, take a step back and assess the situation objectively.

4. **Conduct online research:** Before becoming emotionally invested in someone, conduct online research to see if their identity aligns with what they have shared. Look for inconsistencies, check their social media profiles, and search for any red flags.

5. **Report suspicious behavior:** If you suspect someone is catfishing you or others, report the account to the relevant platform or website administrators. By doing so, you can help protect yourself and others from falling victim to deceptive individuals.

Catfishing is a concerning phenomenon that highlights the risks and challenges associated with online interactions. By maintaining a healthy skepticism, being cautious, and staying informed, individuals can reduce their vulnerability and protect themselves from falling prey to catfishers.

The Techniques behind catfisching
Catfishing is a deceptive practice where someone creates a fake online persona to lure others into a romantic or emotional relationship. Emotional manipulation techniques can vary depending on the individual, but here are some common tactics that catfishers may use:

1. **False empathy:** Catfishers often pretend to deeply understand and empathize with their targets' emotional struggles. They use this technique to gain trust and create a strong emotional bond.

2. **Love bombing:** Catfishers shower their targets with excessive attention, compliments, and expressions of love and affection. This tactic is designed to make the target feel

valued and desired, creating an emotional dependency on the catfisher.

3. **Gaslighting:** Catfishers may manipulate their targets by distorting their perception of reality. They may deny or downplay their deceptive actions, making the target question their own judgment and sanity.

4. **Guilt-tripping:** Manipulators often use guilt as a tool to control their targets. They may invent sob stories or personal tragedies to evoke sympathy and compassion from their victims. This guilt-tripping can make the target feel responsible for the catfisher's well-being and more inclined to comply with their requests.

5. **Isolation:** Catfishers may try to isolate their targets from friends and family, making them believe that others won't understand or approve of their relationship. By cutting off external support systems, catfishers can gain more control over their victims.

6. **Future faking:** Manipulators frequently make grand promises about the future, such as marriage or starting a family together, to keep their targets emotionally invested and hopeful. These promises are often empty and serve as a means to maintain control.

7. **Emotional blackmail:** Catfishers may threaten to reveal personal information or embarrassing details they have learned about their targets during the relationship. This tactic is used to intimidate the target into complying with their demands or keeping the relationship a secret.

It's important to remember that catfishing is a form of manipulation and deception. If you suspect you are being catfished or have concerns about someone you've met online, it's crucial to prioritize your own safety and seek support from trusted friends, family, or professionals.

Romance Scams

Romance scams are a form of fraud in which criminals target individuals through online dating platforms, social media, or email to manipulate their emotions and exploit them financially. These scams can be highly deceptive and devastating for the victims involved. To help you protect yourself, here are some warning signs and red flags that can indicate a romance scam:

1. **Too much, too soon:** Scammers often profess their love or deep affection very quickly, even before meeting in person. They may also try to escalate the relationship rapidly, pushing for commitments or future plans without taking the time to establish a genuine connection.

2. **Unusual profile or backstory:** Scammers often create fake profiles using stolen photos and fictitious personal information. Be cautious if their profile appears too perfect, lacks specific details, or contains inconsistencies in their story. Watch out for profiles with professions like military personnel, oil rig workers, or charity workers, as scammers commonly use these occupations to gain sympathy.

3. **Limited availability for communication:** Scammers may claim to have limited access to technology or internet services due to their job or location, making it difficult to communicate via video calls or in real-time. They might also provide excuses for being unable to meet in person.

4. **Requests for money:** One of the primary goals of romance scammers is to extract money from their victims. They often come up with plausible-sounding reasons to ask for financial assistance, such as medical emergencies, travel expenses, or investments. They may use various tactics to make you feel guilty or obligated to help them.

5. **Inconsistent or evasive behavior:** If the person you're communicating with frequently avoids answering direct questions or provides inconsistent responses, it could be a

red flag. Scammers often dodge personal details and prefer to keep conversations vague to avoid being caught in lies.

6. **Unwillingness to meet in person:** While scammers might offer excuses like distance or financial constraints, they generally try to avoid meeting face-to-face. They may prolong the online relationship, keeping you emotionally invested without any intention of meeting in real life.

7. **Poor grammar and language skills:** Many romance scammers operate from countries where English is not their first language, leading to noticeable grammar and spelling mistakes in their messages. However, it's important to note that some scammers can be quite skilled and may not exhibit this characteristic.

8. **Pressure to move off the dating platform:** Scammers often try to steer communication away from the dating site or app and onto personal email or messaging platforms. This tactic allows them to maintain control and avoid detection by the platform's security measures.

9. **Love bombing:** Scammers frequently shower their victims with excessive compliments, flattery, and expressions of love early on. They use these tactics to manipulate emotions, gain trust, and make the victim more susceptible to their requests.

10. **Lack of social media presence:** Scammers often have limited or nonexistent social media profiles. It's uncommon for someone to have no digital footprint in today's connected world, so be cautious if you can't find any trace of their online presence.

If you notice any of these warning signs or red flags, it's essential to be skeptical and take steps to protect yourself. Trust your instincts, do thorough research on the person you're interacting with, and consider reaching out to friends or family for their perspective.

Additionally, report any suspicious activity or individuals to the relevant authorities and the platform where you encountered them.

Financial requests

When it comes to dating, financial requests and wire transfers should be approached with caution. Here are some important points to keep in mind:

1. **Be skeptical of financial requests:** If someone you're dating asks you for money or financial assistance early in the relationship, it's essential to be cautious. While there may be genuine reasons for financial need, such as an emergency or unexpected situation, it's crucial to verify the legitimacy of the request.

2. **Take your time:** Building trust takes time in any relationship. Be wary of individuals who rush into financial matters or put pressure on you to make quick decisions. Take the time to get to know your partner and establish a solid foundation of trust before considering any financial involvement.

3. **Verify the information:** If your partner asks for financial assistance, make sure to gather as much information as possible. Ask for specific details about the situation and the reasons behind the request. If they claim to be in a dire situation, try to independently verify the information to ensure it's not a scam.

4. **Never share personal financial information:** Protect your personal financial information at all costs. Never share your bank account details, credit card numbers, or any other sensitive information with someone you've just started dating. It's important to prioritize your own financial security.

5. **Be cautious of wire transfers:** Wire transfers can be convenient for sending money quickly, but they can also be risky. Scammers often use wire transfers because they are

difficult to trace and can be irreversible. Exercise caution when asked to make wire transfers, especially to individuals you haven't met in person or haven't established a high level of trust with.

6. **Report suspicious activity:** If you suspect that you're being targeted by a scammer or someone attempting to exploit your finances, report the situation to the appropriate authorities. This helps protect others from falling victim to similar schemes.

Remember, healthy relationships are built on trust, mutual respect, and open communication. While financial assistance can sometimes be a part of a committed relationship, it should be approached cautiously and with careful consideration.

Conducting background research

When it comes to dating, conducting background research can be an important step to ensure your safety and compatibility with the person you're interested in. Here are some guidelines on how to conduct background research when dating:

1. **Online search:** Start by searching for the person's name online. Look for their social media profiles, professional information, and any public records that might be available. This can give you a basic understanding of their background and interests.

2. **Social media investigation:** Examine the person's social media profiles to get more insights into their lifestyle, values, and behavior. Look for any red flags or inconsistencies that may raise concerns. However, keep in mind that not everyone is active on social media, so don't solely rely on this method.

3. **Mutual connections:** If you have any mutual friends or acquaintances, consider reaching out to them discreetly to gather more information about the person. They might be

able to provide you with valuable insights or share their own experiences.

4. **Professional networks:** If the person has a professional presence online, check their LinkedIn profile or other professional networks. This can give you an idea of their work history, qualifications, and connections.

5. **Online background check services:** There are various online background check services available that can provide more comprehensive information about a person's criminal records, public records, and other relevant data. Keep in mind that some of these services may require a fee, and it's important to use reputable sources.

6. **Trust your intuition:** While conducting background research is essential, it's also important to listen to your gut instincts. If something feels off or doesn't add up, it's worth paying attention to those feelings and proceeding with caution.

Remember that background research should be approached with respect for privacy and discretion. It's important not to invade someone's privacy or use the information obtained to harm or judge them unfairly. Background research should be used as a tool to make informed decisions and prioritize your safety when entering a new relationship.

The scale of the problem

The scale of the problem with fake profiles when dating has become a significant concern in the online dating world. With the rise in popularity of dating apps and websites, there has been a corresponding increase in the number of individuals creating fake profiles to deceive and manipulate unsuspecting users.

Fake profiles, also known as catfishing, involve individuals creating fictional personas with fabricated information, photos, and interests to engage with others online. These profiles can be created for various reasons, such as scamming, harassment, or simply seeking attention and validation. Regardless of the motive, the consequences can be emotionally devastating for the victims involved.

One of the primary issues with fake profiles is the erosion of trust within online dating communities. When individuals encounter fake profiles, they may lose faith in the authenticity of other profiles they come across, making it difficult to establish genuine connections. The fear of being deceived can lead to skepticism and reluctance to engage with potential matches, hindering the overall experience and purpose of dating platforms.

Another significant concern with fake profiles is the potential for financial scams. Some individuals create fake profiles to establish relationships with unsuspecting users and then exploit them for financial gain. These scams can range from requesting money for personal emergencies to more elaborate schemes involving investments or fraudulent business opportunities. Victims may find themselves emotionally and financially devastated after falling prey to these manipulative tactics.

Moreover, fake profiles can have severe emotional consequences for those who form attachments with the fabricated personas. Developing feelings for someone who does not exist can lead to heartbreak and emotional trauma. Victims of catfishing may experience a sense of betrayal, humiliation, and a loss of self-esteem. The impact can be long-lasting and can affect future relationships, leading to skepticism and difficulty in trusting others.

Dating platforms have recognized the gravity of the issue and have implemented measures to combat fake profiles. These measures include stringent verification processes, artificial intelligence algorithms that detect suspicious activities and patterns, and user reporting systems. However, despite these efforts, it remains a challenging task to eliminate fake profiles due to the ever-evolving strategies employed by scammers.

To protect oneself from falling victim to fake profiles, it is essential to be cautious and vigilant while engaging in online dating. Some recommended precautions include conducting reverse image searches to verify profile pictures, staying skeptical of individuals who request money or personal information early on, and reporting any suspicious profiles to the platform administrators.

In conclusion, the scale of the problem with fake profiles when dating is a significant issue that affects many individuals seeking love or companionship online. It undermines trust, leads to financial scams, and inflicts emotional distress on victims. While dating platforms continue to improve their security measures, it is crucial for users to remain vigilant and exercise caution when interacting with others online.

Reporting fake profiles and scams
When encountering fake profiles or scams while dating online, it's important to take appropriate actions to protect yourself and others from potential harm. Here are some steps you can follow to report fake profiles and scams:

1. **Document the evidence:** Take screenshots or gather any relevant information that can support your case. This includes messages, profile details, and any suspicious activities you may have noticed.

2. **Report the profile on the dating platform:** Most dating platforms have reporting features to flag fake profiles and scams. Look for options like "Report User" or "Flag Profile" and provide a detailed explanation of your concerns, attaching any evidence you have collected. The platform's support team will review your report and take appropriate action.

3. **Block and cease communication:** If you suspect a profile is fake or involved in a scam, it's best to cut off contact and block the user. Do not engage further or provide any personal or financial information.

4. **Warn others:** If you have identified a scam or fake profile, consider sharing your experience on relevant forums or social media platforms. This can help raise awareness and prevent others from falling victim to similar scams.

5. **Report to authorities:** If you have been a victim of a scam or suspect illegal activity, report it to your local law enforcement agency or the appropriate cybercrime unit. Provide them with all the evidence you have gathered, including any communication or financial transactions.

6. **Use online reporting tools:** Some countries have dedicated online reporting portals for reporting scams and cybercrimes. Research if your country offers such resources and submit your complaint through those channels.

7. **Stay vigilant:** While reporting is crucial, it's also essential to be proactive in protecting yourself. Be cautious when sharing personal information online and when interacting with new people. Educate yourself about common online dating scams to help identify red flags and protect yourself from potential threats.

Remember, reporting fake profiles and scams not only helps you but also assists in maintaining the safety and integrity of online dating platforms.

CHAPTER 4

INTERVIEW YOUR FUTURE PARTNER

CHAPTER 4 – Interview your future partner

Interview your future partner
We also agreed that it's important to make a sincere effort to interview your date, slipping in the right questions to understand their interests and what brings them happiness or sadness in life. I understand that some people might find this approach annoying, but let's consider the success and failure rates of marriages. How many individuals take the time to truly discover their potential partner's interests, what brings them joy or sorrow in life? As someone with a Christian outlook, I would be concerned if I discovered that the person sitting across from me was a devil worshiper. Asking a few questions can hardly do any harm, right?

By delving into your date's interests, you not only gain valuable insights but also demonstrate a genuine interest in them, creating a stronger connection. It's a win-win situation.

I've contemplated the idea of an interview extensively. Should you be transparent about your desire to succeed in your next relationship? Could it be wrong? I don't think so. Put yourself in their shoes; if someone expressed such sincerity to you, wouldn't you feel that it was significant? The only way it could go wrong is if the other person isn't looking for a serious relationship. In that case, both of you can move on without wasting each other's time. The purpose of the list is to find a lifelong partner.

One approach could be to treat this process like a game, doing it together. By laying all the cards on the table from the beginning, topics that are typically challenging to address naturally come to the surface. You and your partner can complete a list together and compare question by question. Try to grade your list from showstoppers to less important.

Interview technique

Interviewing your date in a smart and thoughtful manner can help you gather important information and gain insights about their personality, values, and compatibility. Hopefully you do it in a way so it will not sound like a proper interview of course. Here are some tips on how to conduct a smart interview during a date:

1. **Prepare meaningful questions:** Before the date, take some time to brainstorm and write down a list of questions that are important to you. Focus on topics that can help you understand your date's character, interests, and long-term goals. These could include questions about their passions, values, career aspirations, family dynamics, or views on important topics like relationships, communication, and personal growth.

2. **Active listening:** During the date, be an active listener, yes I say it again. Pay attention to what your date is saying, maintain eye contact, and show genuine interest in their responses. This will not only help you gather information but also demonstrate that you value their thoughts and opinions. Avoid interrupting or formulating your response while they're still speaking—instead, give them the space to express themselves fully.

3. **Balance the conversation:** A successful interview should have a balanced exchange of information. While it's important to ask questions, remember to share about yourself as well. Don't turn the date into an interrogation or monologue. Find a healthy rhythm where both of you have the opportunity to ask and answer questions, creating a comfortable and engaging dialogue.

4. **Use open-ended questions:** Open-ended questions encourage your date to elaborate and provide more detailed answers, fostering deeper conversation. Instead of asking simple yes-or-no questions, try to ask questions that require thoughtful responses. For example, instead of asking, "Do

you like traveling?" you could ask, "What are some of your favorite travel experiences and why?"

5. **Observe non-verbal cues:** Pay attention to your date's body language and non-verbal cues. These can provide valuable insights into their comfort level, interest, and overall demeanor. Notice if they maintain eye contact, lean in while listening, or display signs of discomfort or disinterest. Non-verbal cues can give you a better understanding of how they are feeling and if there is alignment between their words and actions.

6. **Trust your intuition:** While conducting a smart interview is important, it's equally essential to trust your intuition and gut feelings. If something feels off or inconsistent, take note of it. Listen to your inner voice and evaluate whether the information you're gathering aligns with your own values and relationship goals. Don't dismiss any red flags or concerns that arise during the conversation.

7. **Reflect and evaluate:** After the date, take some time to reflect on the information you gathered and evaluate how it aligns with your own values, needs, and long-term goals. Consider whether the conversation left you feeling heard, respected, and understood. This reflection can help you make an informed decision about pursuing further dates or exploring a potential relationship.

Remember, while interviewing your date can provide valuable insights, it's important to balance it with organic conversation and genuine connection. Allow the date to flow naturally and enjoy getting to know each other in an authentic way.

The falling in love syndrome
The feeling of falling in love when dating is often described as an intense and euphoric experience. It's a combination of emotional,

physiological, and psychological responses that occur when you develop strong romantic feelings for someone.

When you find yourself falling in love...
Discovering your desires, creating a checklist, engaging in meaningful conversations – why are these steps so significant? When love takes hold, it renders us defenseless, rendering any list irrelevant. The love we encounter, ideally, is the most formidable force we can expose ourselves to. Amidst this exhilaration, there is no room for checklists, and our partner's imperfections fade away, leaving us with a rosy perception. However, the intensity of love will eventually wane. Perhaps not tomorrow, maybe not even in a year, but rest assured, a moment will come when your partner stands before you in flesh and blood, flaws exposed under the daylight's gaze.

Suddenly, the checklist becomes relevant once again. Now, the partner is real, devoid of any rose-colored lenses. How comforting it is to have everything aligned, no insurmountable obstacles, shared interests, and the ideal conditions for a remarkable relationship. Therefore, it is crucial to have your list in place before love fully engulfs you, while you can still objectively observe the person sitting across from you.

When you meet someone, you're attracted to and start dating, several factors contribute to the falling in love syndrome:

1. **Chemical reactions:** Falling in love involves a surge of chemicals in the brain, including dopamine, oxytocin, and serotonin. These chemicals create feelings of pleasure, happiness, and attachment, which can lead to a sense of euphoria and excitement.

2. **Emotional connection:** As you spend time with someone and get to know them better, you may develop a deep emotional connection. This connection can involve sharing personal experiences, opening up about your feelings, and feeling understood and supported by the other person. This

emotional intimacy strengthens the bond between you and contributes to the falling in love experience.

3. **Idealization:** In the early stages of dating, it's common to idealize the person you're interested in. You may focus on their positive qualities, overlook flaws, and have a heightened sense of admiration and infatuation. This idealization can contribute to the intense feelings associated with falling in love.

4. **Shared experiences:** Engaging in activities together, going on dates, and creating shared memories can foster a sense of intimacy and connection. These shared experiences contribute to the development of a strong emotional bond and reinforce the feelings of falling in love.

5. **Physical attraction:** Physical attraction plays a significant role in the falling in love experience. The initial spark and chemistry you feel with someone can lead to a heightened sense of desire and passion, which can intensify the emotional connection.

It's important to note that the falling in love syndrome can vary from person to person and relationship to relationship. While some people may experience it quickly and intensely, others may take more time to develop strong feelings. It's also worth mentioning that the initial infatuation and excitement of falling in love may fade over time, transitioning into a more stable and mature love based on deeper emotional connections and shared values.

Showstopper!
When me and my friend was talking about our past partners our collective thoughts led us to believe that a greater similarity between partners leads to greater chances of success. Over time, the differences wear down the relationship more than they benefit it. It was during this conversation that "The List" was conceived. This list serves as a set of criteria, outlining the interests and qualities

we desire in our partners. Oh, how we indulged in our fantasies! In no time, my list grew to over eleven points, while Robin's reached fifteen. We shared our lists and burst into laughter. How on earth could anyone find a person who embodies all these qualities? We quickly acknowledged the impossibility of such perfection, even within ourselves. Our entire theory of having a checklist to tick off when meeting someone crumbled before our eyes.

Nobody is perfect

In realizing that perfection eludes everyone, including ourselves, we embarked on a discussion of our respective imperfections. It became clear that certain points carried more weight than others as we deliberated. Recognizing the varying degrees of importance, we decided to grade and prioritize our list. This process enabled us to discern which aspects were truly vital and which ones we could potentially forgo.

As we evaluated, we naturally identified elements of immense significance—those integral to our very being, such as core values, personal principles, and fundamental needs. These constituted the bedrock upon which we constructed our identities, shaping our actions and choices.

Simultaneously, we acknowledged the presence of items on our list that held lesser importance—preferences, desires, or aspects that, while valuable, were not indispensable to our overall sense of fulfillment. Understanding the elusive nature of perfection, we recognized the inevitability of compromises and the need to accommodate differences as inherent to human relationships. Our list began to evolve accordingly.

Top 3 criteria

Our priorities have shifted dramatically. Following a recent evaluation, it became evident that if a potential partner fails to meet the "top 3" criteria, it becomes an insurmountable obstacle - a showstopper. Allow me to provide some examples: Let's say I have a deep passion for traveling, yet the person I'm interested in has no inclination for exploration and prefers to remain homebound. The mere thought of relinquishing such a cherished interest is inconceivable to me. Without a doubt, this misalignment becomes a showstopper, rendering a successful relationship unattainable. Therefore, if during interactions with a potential partner, I observe a discrepancy in one of the three most crucial aspects, it is imperative to terminate the connection before it takes root. According to our theory, it is only a matter of time before irreconcilable differences lead to its demise.

In some instances, it can be quite disconcerting as I delve into hypothetical scenarios. Is it plausible for a particular attribute, initially ranked seventh on the list, to rise in significance over time? You see, your partner might exhibit a certain behavior that, while initially trivial, becomes increasingly exasperating with each passing day. Could this be a possibility? It's undoubtedly a gamble!

I, too, have my own set of irksome factors. For instance, I cannot tolerate the sound of someone eating with their mouth open. Even during my childhood, it was a constant source of contention between my brother and me. He would deliberately amplify the smacking noise to tease me. Often, this led to wrestling matches, at best. I have made my stance clear on this matter with my children as well, and unfortunately, they have developed the same aversion to such behavior. As my eldest daughter once remarked, I could never be with a person who habitually eats with their mouth open. Imagine if my wife had been an avid smacker - our marriage might not have materialized, undoubtedly a showstopper for me.

One can continue ad infinitum, contemplating what irks them. It is crucial to reflect on these irritants. Certain behaviors that trigger annoyance and are intolerable, such as open-mouthed chewing in my case, can indeed be addressed with a prospective partner. However, it may feel somewhat awkward to broach such subjects on the second date, wouldn't you agree? Yet, if love blossoms, such behaviors should be open to correction.

Can we guard against hidden showstoppers? We now delve into aspects that do not currently bother us in the blissful state of infatuation but tend to escalate over time. Here, we return to the concept of our list. If it is a priority on our list, it naturally possesses the potential to gain prominence. However, we must be prepared to live with it. During the initial stages of a relationship, the utmost priority is to eliminate deal-breakers - those things we absolutely cannot tolerate. It is essential to embark on a relationship with eyes wide open. It may seem self-centered, but it is our own lives at stake. As I mentioned earlier, life is too short to settle for anything less than our first choice. We should strive for the best and dare to establish what is most important to us without factoring in our potential partner's desires.

CHAPTER 5

THE ART OF COMMUNICATION

CHAPTER 5 – The art of communication

Developing effective communication skills

Developing effective communication skills is essential for successful dating. Clear and open communication helps build a strong foundation of understanding, trust, and connection between two individuals. Whether you're getting to know someone for the first time or have been dating for a while, honing your communication skills can greatly enhance your dating experiences. Here are some tips to help you develop effective communication skills for dating:

1. **Active Listening:** It's a reason why you will see in these book that active listening is repeated and again. Listening is one of the most important parts to have a good relationship. So, pay attention to what your date is saying, not just their words, but also their body language and tone of voice. Engage in active listening by maintaining eye contact, nodding, and asking follow-up questions. This shows genuine interest and helps your date feel heard and understood.

2. **Express Yourself Clearly:** Be clear and concise when expressing your thoughts and feelings. Avoid using vague or ambiguous language that can lead to misunderstandings. Use "I" statements to express your emotions and opinions, as it takes ownership of your thoughts rather than blaming or accusing your date.

3. **Nonverbal Communication:** Remember that communication extends beyond words. Pay attention to your body language, facial expressions, and gestures. Maintain good posture, smile, and use appropriate touch (if comfortable and consensual) to convey interest and affection.

4. **Emotional Intelligence:** Develop emotional intelligence by being aware of your own emotions and those of your date. Recognize and manage your emotions effectively and try to empathize with your date's feelings. Emotional intelligence

allows you to respond empathetically and navigate potential conflicts or disagreements with understanding and compassion.

5. **Be Respectful:** Treat your date with respect by listening without interrupting, avoiding judgment or criticism, and valuing their opinions and perspectives. Respectful communication creates an environment of trust and mutual understanding.

6. **Practice Assertiveness:** Be assertive in expressing your needs, boundaries, and desires. It's important to communicate your expectations and be honest about what you want from the relationship. This helps avoid misunderstandings and promotes healthy communication.

7. **Mindful Communication:** Practice mindfulness in your conversations. Be fully present in the moment, giving your undivided attention to your date. Minimize distractions such as phone use and show genuine interest in what they have to say. I Think it's good to repeat, put the phone away when you meet face to face.

8. **Resolve Conflicts Constructively:** Disagreements and conflicts are natural in any relationship. When conflicts arise, address them in a constructive and respectful manner. Avoid blame and focus on finding solutions together. Use "we" instead of "you" or "I" to emphasize that you're a team working towards resolution.

9. **Learn from Feedback:** Be open to feedback from your date and use it as an opportunity for personal growth. Constructive feedback helps you understand your strengths and areas for improvement in communication. Accept feedback gracefully and make an effort to work on any identified areas.

10. **Practice Patience:** Building effective communication skills takes time and practice. Be patient with yourself and your

date as you both learn to communicate effectively and understand each other better. Allow space for growth and be willing to adapt your communication style as the relationship progresses.

Remember that effective communication is a two-way street. It requires active participation and effort from both individuals involved in the dating process. By developing these skills, you can create a strong foundation for healthy, meaningful connections and increase your chances of building a successful relationship.

Active Listening and Expressing Your Needs When Dating
In the realm of dating, effective communication is vital for building meaningful connections and establishing a strong foundation. Two essential aspects of communication in dating are active listening and expressing your needs. These skills play a crucial role in understanding your partner, fostering trust, and nurturing a healthy and fulfilling relationship.

Active listening is a technique that involves fully engaging with your partner's words, nonverbal cues, and emotions during a conversation. It goes beyond simply hearing what they say and delves into truly understanding their perspective and feelings. Here are a few key elements of active listening:

1. **Paying attention:** When your partner speaks, give them your full attention. Maintain eye contact, avoid distractions, and focus on their words. This shows respect and demonstrates your genuine interest in what they have to say.

2. **Nonverbal cues:** Apart from words, pay attention to your partner's body language, facial expressions, and tone of voice. These nonverbal cues can convey additional information about their emotions and help you understand their underlying feelings.

3. **Reflecting and clarifying:** Active listening involves periodically paraphrasing or summarizing what your partner has said to ensure you've understood them correctly. This reflection not only shows that you're actively engaged but also gives your partner an opportunity to clarify any misunderstandings.

4. **Empathy and validation:** Try to put yourself in your partner's shoes and understand their perspective. Show empathy by acknowledging their emotions and validating their experiences. This helps create a safe and supportive environment for open communication.

Once you have actively listened and understood your partner's thoughts and feelings, it's crucial to express your own needs as well. Effective communication is a two-way street, and expressing your needs ensures that your boundaries, desires, and expectations are understood. Here are some tips for expressing your needs:

1. **Self-awareness:** Before you can express your needs, it's essential to be clear about what they are. Take time to reflect on your values, priorities, and relationship goals. Understanding yourself better will help you communicate your needs more effectively.

2. **Timing and context:** Choose an appropriate time and setting to express your needs. Make sure both you and your partner are in a calm and receptive state, free from distractions or time constraints. This allows for a more focused and meaningful conversation.

3. **Use "I" statements:** When expressing your needs, frame your statements using "I" instead of "you." This helps avoid sounding accusatory or confrontational. For example, say, "I feel..." or "I would appreciate it if..." instead of "You always..." or "You never...".

4. **Be specific and constructive:** Clearly articulate your needs, desires, and boundaries. Avoid vague statements and provide specific examples or suggestions when discussing potential solutions. This helps your partner understand your perspective better and promotes open dialogue.

5. **Active listening in return:** Remember that effective communication is a two-way process. Encourage your partner to actively listen to your needs and respond with empathy and understanding. Just as you listened to them, expect the same level of engagement and respect.

By actively listening to your partner and expressing your needs in a considerate manner, you foster an environment of open and honest communication. These skills promote understanding, build trust, and enhance the overall quality of your dating experience. Remember, effective communication is a continuous practice that strengthens connections and paves the way for a healthy and fulfilling relationship.

Navigating conflicts and resolving differences

Navigating conflicts and resolving differences is an essential part of any relationship, including dating. Here are some tips to help you handle conflicts and resolve differences effectively:

1. **Open and honest communication:** Communication is key to resolving conflicts. Express your thoughts, feelings, and concerns openly and honestly, and encourage your partner to do the same. Active listening is equally important—make an effort to understand each other's perspectives without interrupting or becoming defensive.

2. **Choose the right time and place:** Timing and environment can significantly impact the outcome of a discussion. Pick a suitable time when both of you are calm and can focus on the conversation. Choose a neutral location where you can have privacy and minimize distractions.

3. **Seek understanding, not victory:** Remember that conflicts should not be about winning or proving the other person wrong. Instead, focus on understanding each other's viewpoints and finding common ground. Practice empathy and try to see things from your partner's perspective.

4. **Compromise and find common solutions:** Look for solutions that meet both of your needs. Identify areas where you can compromise and find middle ground. It's essential to be flexible and willing to make adjustments for the sake of the relationship.

5. **Respect boundaries and emotions:** Be mindful of each other's boundaries and emotional well-being during conflicts. Avoid personal attacks, name-calling, or bringing up past grievances. Treat each other with respect, even when you disagree.

6. **Seek external support if needed:** Sometimes, conflicts can be challenging to resolve on your own. Consider seeking the help of a neutral third party, such as a couples therapist or a trusted friend or family member, who can offer guidance and facilitate productive discussions.

7. **Learn from conflicts:** Conflicts can be opportunities for growth and understanding. Reflect on the underlying causes of the conflict and learn from them. Use the experience to strengthen your relationship and develop better communication skills.

Remember, conflicts are normal in any relationship. How you handle them can make a significant difference in the health and longevity of your relationship. By practicing effective communication, empathy, and a willingness to find common ground, you can navigate conflicts and resolve differences in a constructive and respectful manner.

CHAPTER 6

THE FIRST DATE

CHAPTER 6 - The First Date

Preparing for a successful first date

Preparing for a successful first date can be an exciting yet nerve-wracking experience. It's natural to feel a mix of anticipation and anxiety, as you want to make a positive impression on your potential partner. While there is no foolproof formula for the perfect first date, there are several steps you can take to increase the likelihood of a successful and enjoyable experience. Here are some tips to help you prepare for a memorable first date:

1. **Plan ahead:** Take the time to plan the date in advance. Consider your date's interests, preferences, and any conversations you've had leading up to the date. Choose a location or activity that both of you will enjoy and feel comfortable with. It could be a cozy coffee shop, a scenic park, or trying out a new restaurant. Planning ahead shows thoughtfulness and consideration, which can set a positive tone for the date.

2. **Dress appropriately:** It sounds stupid to say it, but I say it anyway, make an effort to dress appropriately for the occasion. While it's essential to feel comfortable, dressing slightly more formal or put-together than your everyday attire can demonstrate that you value the occasion and your date's company. Dressing well also boosts your own confidence, allowing you to feel your best throughout the evening.

3. **Be punctual:** Arriving on time is a sign of respect and consideration for your date's time. Aim to be punctual or even a few minutes early. It helps create a positive first impression and avoids any unnecessary stress or disappointment caused by lateness.

4. **Be yourself:** Authenticity is key on a first date. Be genuine and true to yourself. While it's natural to feel nervous, try to

relax and engage in meaningful conversations. Be attentive, ask questions, and actively listen to your date. Sharing your thoughts, experiences, and interests will help create a connection and make the date more enjoyable for both of you.

5. **Keep the conversation light:** While it's important to get to know each other, avoid heavy or controversial topics on the first date. Instead, focus on light-hearted and fun conversations. Talk about hobbies, favorite books or movies, travel experiences, or any shared interests you have discovered. This approach encourages a relaxed atmosphere and allows both of you to enjoy the conversation without feeling overwhelmed.

6. **Maintain positive body language:** Nonverbal cues can convey a lot about your attitude and interest. Maintain good eye contact, smile genuinely, and use open body language to signal that you are engaged and enjoying the company. Avoid distractions like checking your phone or looking around the room, as it may give the impression that you are not fully present.

7. **Show appreciation:** A simple "thank you" or compliment can go a long way in making your date feel appreciated. Acknowledge their efforts, such as choosing the venue or organizing the date. Express genuine interest and appreciation for their company and be polite and respectful throughout the evening.

8. **Be prepared for unexpected outcomes:** While you may hope for a perfect first date, it's important to keep in mind that not every interaction will lead to a romantic connection. Be open-minded and understanding, regardless of the outcome. Even if there is no romantic spark, you can still enjoy a pleasant evening and potentially build a new friendship.

Remember, the most successful first dates are those where both parties feel comfortable, enjoy each other's company, and establish a genuine connection. So, relax, be yourself, and embrace the opportunity to get to know someone new. By the way, you can use my tips above in any job interview to.

Conversation starters and icebreakers
Conversation starters and icebreakers play a crucial role in dating scenarios, as they can help establish a connection and create a relaxed and enjoyable atmosphere between two individuals. When it comes to dating, it's important to choose conversation starters that are light-hearted, engaging, and enable both parties to share about themselves. Here are some effective conversation starters and icebreakers for dating:

1. **Ask about shared interests:** Begin by asking about hobbies, passions, or activities that you both enjoy. For example, "I noticed in your profile that you enjoy hiking. What's your favorite hiking spot and why?"

2. **Discuss favorite movies, TV shows, or books:** Pop culture is often a great topic for conversation. You can ask questions like, "What's the last movie you watched that made you laugh out loud?" or "Do you have any book recommendations? I'm looking for something new to read."

3. **Travel experiences:** Share and discuss memorable travel experiences or dream destinations. Ask questions like, "What's the most adventurous trip you've been on?" or "If you could travel anywhere in the world, where would you go and why?"

4. **Food and culinary preferences:** Food is a universal topic that can spark interesting conversations. Ask about their favorite cuisine, restaurants they love, or even their go-to comfort food. You could say, "Are you more of a sweet or

savory person when it comes to food?" or "What's the best meal you've ever had?"

5. **Childhood memories:** Discussing childhood memories can evoke nostalgia and create a sense of intimacy. You can ask questions like, "What was your favorite childhood game or toy?" or "Did you have any funny or memorable family traditions when you were growing up?"

6. **Share funny stories:** Sharing humorous anecdotes can help lighten the mood and create a positive connection. You could say, "I have this embarrassing story from my college days. Mind if I share it?" or "What's the funniest thing that has ever happened to you?"

Remember, the goal of conversation starters and icebreakers when dating is to establish a comfortable and engaging dialogue. Be an attentive listener, show genuine interest, and be open to sharing about yourself as well. Ultimately, these conversation techniques are meant to facilitate a connection between two individuals, allowing them to explore common interests and experiences while enjoying each other's company.

Navigating awkward moments and building chemistry
Navigating awkward moments and building chemistry when dating can be both exciting and challenging. It's natural to experience some discomfort and uncertainty when getting to know someone new, but with the right approach and mindset, you can turn those awkward moments into opportunities for building a genuine connection. Here are some tips to help you navigate those awkward moments and cultivate chemistry while dating:

1. **Embrace the awkwardness:** Acknowledge that awkward moments are a normal part of the dating process. Everyone experiences them to some extent, and they often arise from a desire to make a good impression. By embracing the

awkwardness, you can diffuse tension and create a more relaxed atmosphere.

2. **Maintain a positive attitude:** A positive mindset can work wonders in awkward situations. Instead of dwelling on the discomfort, focus on the potential for growth and connection. Remember that awkward moments can be endearing and even bring you closer together if both parties handle them with humor and grace.

3. **Practice active listening:** Engage in active listening during your conversations. Show genuine interest in your date's stories, experiences, and perspectives. Maintain eye contact, nod, and ask follow-up questions. By demonstrating that you're fully present and engaged, you create a space for connection and chemistry to flourish.

4. **Use humor to diffuse tension:** Humor can be a powerful tool in navigating awkward moments. Light-hearted jokes or playful banter can help break the ice and alleviate tension. However, be mindful of your date's sense of humor and the context, ensuring your jokes are appropriate and well-received.

5. **Be authentic and vulnerable:** Building chemistry requires openness and vulnerability. Allow yourself to be genuine and share your thoughts, feelings, and experiences. By being authentic, you create an environment where your date feels comfortable doing the same, fostering a deeper connection between you.

6. **Pay attention to body language:** Nonverbal cues play a significant role in building chemistry. Pay attention to your date's body language, as well as your own. Smile, maintain open posture, and mirror positive gestures. Subtle touches, such as a light brush on the arm, can also create a sense of connection when appropriate.

7. **Find common interests and activities:** Discover shared interests and engage in activities that you both enjoy. Shared experiences can provide a natural platform for building chemistry. Whether it's trying a new restaurant, going for a hike, or attending a concert, engaging in activities together can help create memorable moments and strengthen your bond.

8. **Practice empathy and understanding:** Dating involves two individuals with different backgrounds, perspectives, and communication styles. Practice empathy and understanding, seeking to see things from your date's point of view. Be patient and compassionate and give each other the benefit of the doubt. This approach fosters an environment of acceptance and mutual respect, promoting chemistry and connection.

9. **Be patient and give it time:** Chemistry is not something that can be forced or rushed. It often develops gradually as you get to know each other better. Be patient and give the relationship time to grow. Allow yourself and your date the space to discover if there's genuine chemistry and compatibility between you.

Remember that dating is a journey, and not every interaction will lead to a deep connection. It's important to be kind to yourself and to your date throughout the process. By embracing the awkward moments, staying open, and fostering genuine connection, you increase the chances of building meaningful chemistry with someone special.

CHAPTER 7

BUILDNING HEALTHY
RELATIONSHIPS

CHAPTER 7 - Building Healthy Relationships

The importance of trust, respect, and open communication

When it comes to dating, trust, respect, and open communication are vital components that contribute to the foundation of a healthy and fulfilling relationship. These qualities create an environment of understanding, connection, and emotional safety, fostering a strong bond between partners. Let's explore the importance of each element in the context of dating.

1. **Trust:** Trust is the cornerstone of any successful relationship. It involves having faith in your partner's honesty, reliability, and intentions. In the dating phase, trust allows individuals to feel secure and comfortable, enabling them to open up emotionally and be vulnerable with each other. Without trust, doubts and insecurities can erode the relationship, leading to misunderstandings and conflicts. Building trust requires consistency, transparency, and the willingness to honor commitments. Trusting each other sets the stage for a strong, lasting connection.

2. **Respect:** Respect is fundamental in dating as it acknowledges and values the worth of each person involved. It entails recognizing and appreciating the individuality, boundaries, and autonomy of your partner. When respect is present, both individuals feel heard, validated, and understood. Respecting each other's opinions, choices, and values fosters a sense of equality and builds a solid foundation for a healthy partnership. Without respect, communication can become dismissive, judgmental, or manipulative, leading to a breakdown in the relationship. Cultivating respect demonstrates a genuine regard for one another, creating an atmosphere of mutual admiration and support.

3. **Open Communication:** Open communication forms the bridge between partners, allowing them to express their thoughts, feelings, needs, and concerns. It involves

actively listening, being honest, and sharing openly without fear of judgment or rejection. In the dating phase, open communication enables both individuals to learn about each other, understand each other's perspectives, and build emotional intimacy. It also encourages the resolution of conflicts through constructive dialogue and compromise. Without open communication, misunderstandings can arise, emotions can be suppressed, and resentment can build up. By fostering open and honest conversations, partners can establish a strong connection, strengthen their bond, and build trust.

In conclusion, trust, respect, and open communication are essential elements in dating. These qualities create a solid foundation for a healthy, fulfilling, and long-lasting relationship. They promote understanding, emotional safety, and a deep sense of connection between partners. By cultivating trust, respect, and open communication, individuals can navigate the challenges of dating with empathy, compassion, and a willingness to grow together.

Nurturing emotional intimacy and vulnerability
Building emotional intimacy and vulnerability is crucial for a healthy and fulfilling romantic relationship. When dating someone new, it's essential to create a safe and nurturing environment where both individuals can open up and connect on a deep emotional level. Here are some suggestions on how to nurture emotional intimacy and vulnerability when dating:

1. **Establish Trust:** Trust is the foundation of emotional intimacy. Honesty, reliability, and consistency are key factors in building trust. Be open and transparent with your partner and honor your commitments and promises. Show that you are dependable and can be relied upon.

2. **Listening:** Listening actively demonstrates that you value your partner's thoughts, feelings, and experiences. Give your undivided attention, maintain eye contact, and avoid

interrupting. Validate their emotions and provide support. Engage in empathetic listening, where you try to understand their perspective without judgment.

3. **Share Personal Experiences:** Opening up about your own experiences and emotions encourages your partner to do the same. Share your fears, hopes, and dreams. Be vulnerable and honest about your past and present struggles. This authenticity fosters a sense of connection and encourages your partner to reciprocate.

4. **Practice Emotional Availability:** Show that you are emotionally available and receptive to your partner's needs. Be empathetic and responsive when they share their emotions. Offer comfort, encouragement, and validation. Make it clear that you are a safe space for them to express themselves without fear of judgment or rejection.

5. **Create a Judgment-Free Zone:** Foster an environment where vulnerability is celebrated, and judgment is absent. Avoid criticizing or shaming your partner for their emotions or vulnerabilities. Instead, offer support and understanding. Accept them for who they are, flaws and all, and encourage them to do the same for you.

6. **Build Gradually:** Emotional intimacy takes time to develop. Allow the relationship to progress naturally and avoid rushing the process. Gradually reveal deeper layers of yourself as trust and connection deepen. Be patient and understanding, honoring each other's pace.

7. **Respect Boundaries:** Everyone has different comfort levels when it comes to emotional vulnerability. Respect your partner's boundaries and don't push them to share more than they are ready for. Creating a safe space means allowing them to open up at their own pace.

8. **Communicate Openly:** Effective communication is essential for nurturing emotional intimacy. Encourage open and honest dialogue, where both partners can express their thoughts, feelings, and needs without fear of judgment or retaliation. Be willing to have difficult conversations, and actively work on conflict resolution together.

9. **Mutual Support:** Show up for your partner and provide emotional support when they need it. Offer encouragement, reassurance, and a listening ear during challenging times. Be empathetic and understanding, helping them navigate their emotions and offering assistance when necessary.

10. **Practice Empathy:** Empathy is the ability to understand and share the feelings of another person. Cultivate empathy by putting yourself in your partner's shoes and trying to understand their perspective. Acknowledge their emotions and respond with compassion.

Remember, building emotional intimacy and vulnerability is an ongoing process that requires effort and commitment from both partners. By creating a safe and nurturing space, actively listening, sharing personal experiences, and practicing empathy, you can foster a deep emotional connection that strengthens your relationship.

Setting boundaries and maintaining independence

Setting boundaries and maintaining independence are vital aspects of a healthy and balanced dating relationship. While it's natural to feel deeply connected to your partner, it's equally important to preserve your own identity and protect your personal well-being. Here are some suggestions on how to set boundaries and maintain independence when dating:

1. **Reflect on Your Needs:** Take the time to understand your own needs, desires, and limits. Reflect on what makes you feel comfortable and fulfilled in a relationship. Consider your emotional, physical, and mental boundaries.

This self-awareness will guide you in establishing healthy boundaries.

2. **Communicate Clearly:** Open and honest communication is key to setting boundaries effectively. Clearly express your needs, expectations, and limitations to your partner. Be assertive and confident when discussing these topics. Remember that your boundaries are valid and deserving of respect.

3. **Be Consistent:** Consistency is crucial when it comes to maintaining boundaries. Enforce your boundaries consistently and ensure that your partner understands the importance of respecting them. This will help establish a sense of trust and reliability in the relationship.

4. **Recognize Warning Signs:** Be vigilant about recognizing any red flags or behaviors that violate your boundaries. If your partner repeatedly disregards or dismisses your boundaries, it may be a sign of an unhealthy dynamic. Trust your instincts and take necessary actions to protect yourself.

5. **Preserve Personal Space:** It's essential to maintain your individuality and personal space in a relationship. Set aside time for your own hobbies, interests, and friendships. Encourage your partner to do the same. This allows for personal growth and prevents co-dependency.

6. **Prioritize Self-Care:** Make self-care a priority in your life. Take care of your physical, emotional, and mental well-being. Engage in activities that recharge and nourish you. By investing in yourself, you bring your best self to the relationship and maintain your independence.

7. **Seek Support Outside the Relationship:** It's healthy to have a support network outside of your romantic partnership. Maintain close relationships with friends and family. Seek advice, guidance, and emotional support from trusted

individuals. This network provides additional perspectives and strengthens your independence.

8. **Embrace Solo Activities:** Engage in activities and experiences that you enjoy on your own. Pursue your passions, hobbies, and goals independently. This not only enhances your personal growth but also strengthens your sense of self.

9. **Establish Mutual Respect:** Mutual respect is the foundation for maintaining independence. Ensure that both you and your partner respect each other's boundaries, personal space, and individuality. Encourage each other's growth and support each other's pursuits outside the relationship.

10. **Revisit and Adjust Boundaries:** As the relationship evolves, it's essential to revisit and adjust boundaries when necessary. Be open to discussing and renegotiating boundaries as both you and your partner grow and change. Flexibility and understanding contribute to a healthy and balanced relationship.

Remember, setting boundaries and maintaining independence is not about creating distance or disengaging from your partner. It's about preserving your own well-being, identity, and personal growth within the context of a loving and respectful relationship. By clearly communicating, prioritizing self-care, and respecting each other's boundaries, you can foster a strong, independent, and fulfilling partnership.

CHAPTER 8

OVERCOMING CHALLENGES

CHAPTER 8 - Overcoming challenges

Dealing with rejection and building resilience
Dealing with rejection and building resilience when dating can be challenging, as it often involves navigating through a range of emotions and uncertainties. Rejection is a natural part of the dating process, and while it may sting, it also presents an opportunity for personal growth and resilience-building. Here are some strategies to help you handle rejection and cultivate resilience in the realm of dating:

1. **Acknowledge and process your emotions**: It's normal to feel disappointed, hurt, or even frustrated when faced with rejection. Allow yourself to experience these emotions and acknowledge them without judgment. It's essential to give yourself time to heal and process before moving forward.

2. **Maintain a positive mindset:** While rejection may feel personal, it's crucial to remember that it's often not about you as an individual. People have their preferences, circumstances, and reasons for their decisions. Instead of dwelling on negative thoughts, focus on maintaining a positive outlook and reminding yourself that rejection is merely part of the dating process.

3. **Learn from the experience:** Rejection can offer valuable lessons if you're open to learning from them. Reflect on the situation and try to identify any patterns or behaviors that may have contributed to the rejection. Use this self-awareness to grow and improve, whether it's in terms of communication skills, self-confidence, or understanding your own needs and wants.

4. **Don't take it personally:** Rejection in dating does not define your worth as an individual. It's essential to separate your self-worth from external validation. Remember that compatibility

and chemistry are subjective, and someone's rejection does not diminish your value or potential for future connections.

5. **Seek support from friends and loved ones:** During challenging times, it's helpful to lean on your support system. Reach out to trusted friends or family members who can provide a listening ear, offer advice, or simply be there for you. Talking about your feelings can provide relief and perspective, helping you regain your confidence and resilience.

6. **Take care of yourself:** Engage in self-care activities that promote well-being and self-love. Focus on nurturing your physical, emotional, and mental health. This may include exercising, pursuing hobbies, practicing mindfulness or meditation, or seeking therapy if needed. Prioritizing self-care will help you bounce back stronger and maintain a positive mindset.

7. **Stay open to new possibilities:** Rejection can sometimes feel like a roadblock, but it's important not to let it discourage you from continuing to explore new connections. Stay open-minded and approach dating with a sense of curiosity and adventure. Remember that each interaction is an opportunity to learn more about yourself and others, and to potentially find a meaningful connection.

8. **Set realistic expectations:** It's important to have realistic expectations when it comes to dating. Not every encounter will result in a long-term relationship, and that's okay. Recognize that rejection is a natural part of the process and that finding the right person often takes time. By managing your expectations, you can approach dating with a healthier mindset and build resilience along the way.

Remember, building resilience takes time and effort. Each rejection is an opportunity for growth and self-discovery. By adopting a positive mindset, learning from your experiences, and taking care of yourself, you can navigate the dating world with greater confidence and resilience.

Managing long distance relationship
Managing long-distance relationships while dating can be both challenging and rewarding. The distance between partners can pose various obstacles, such as limited physical interaction, communication difficulties, and feelings of loneliness. However, with dedication, effective communication, and trust, it's possible to navigate the challenges and maintain a healthy and fulfilling long-distance relationship.

Here are some tips for successfully managing a long-distance relationship while dating:

1. **Communication is key:** Open and honest communication is the foundation of any successful relationship, especially when distance is involved. Make sure to establish regular communication patterns that work for both partners. This may include phone calls, video chats, texting, or even sending letters or care packages. Find a balance that suits your schedules and helps you stay connected.

2. **Set clear expectations:** Discuss and establish expectations regarding the relationship. This includes topics such as commitment, exclusivity, and future plans. Having a shared understanding of where the relationship is headed can help both partners feel secure and reduce any uncertainties that distance may bring.

3. **Utilize technology:** Thankfully, we live in a digital age where technology can bridge the physical gap between partners. Take advantage of video calls, instant messaging, social media, and other online tools to connect and share experiences. Virtual dates, watching movies or TV shows together, and playing online games can help create shared moments and maintain a sense of togetherness.

4. **Plan visits and meet-ups:** Regular visits and meet-ups are essential for strengthening the bond in a long-distance relationship. Schedule visits in advance to give both partners something to look forward to. Planning trips together and exploring new places can create lasting memories and deepen your connection. However, it's important to manage expectations and be realistic about the frequency and duration of visits based on practical considerations such as finances and work obligations.

5. **Build trust:** Trust is vital in any relationship, but it becomes even more crucial in a long-distance one. Be open, honest, and transparent with each other. Avoid keeping secrets or hiding information, as this can lead to doubts and insecurities. Trust your partner and give them the benefit of the doubt. Establishing trust creates a solid foundation and allows the relationship to flourish.

6. **Pursue personal goals and interests:** While it's important to invest time and effort into the relationship, it's equally essential to maintain individuality. Pursuing personal goals, hobbies, and interests not only keeps you occupied but also enhances personal growth. Encourage your partner to do the same. Sharing your accomplishments and experiences will give you both something positive to discuss and strengthen the bond between you.

7. **Be supportive and understanding:** Long-distance relationships can be emotionally challenging at times. Understand that your partner may have difficult days, feel lonely, or struggle with the distance. Offer emotional support and be understanding of their needs. It's important to be patient, empathetic, and validate their feelings. Creating a safe space for open communication allows both partners to express their emotions without judgment.

8. **Maintain a positive outlook:** Long-distance relationships require optimism and positivity. Focus on the future and

the shared goals you are working towards. Celebrate small milestones and achievements together. A positive attitude can help overcome the challenges of distance and keep the relationship thriving.

Remember that managing a long-distance relationship takes effort, commitment, and compromise from both partners. Despite the challenges, a well-nurtured long-distance relationship can lead to a stronger bond, deeper emotional connection, and personal growth.

Handling cultural and religious differences

Handling cultural and religious differences when dating can be both challenging and rewarding. It requires open-mindedness, respect, and effective communication to build a strong foundation for a successful relationship. Here are some key considerations and strategies for navigating these differences:

1. **Respect and Understanding:** It is essential to approach cultural and religious differences with respect and genuine curiosity. Take the time to learn about your partner's background, beliefs, customs, and practices. Be open to understanding their perspectives and experiences, and avoid making assumptions or stereotypes.

2. **Open Communication:** Clear and open communication is crucial in any relationship, especially when dealing with cultural and religious differences. Discuss your beliefs, values, and traditions with each other to gain a deeper understanding of your backgrounds. Be prepared to listen actively and empathetically, expressing your thoughts and concerns honestly and respectfully.

3. **Flexibility and Compromise:** Recognize that compromises may be necessary to accommodate both partners' cultural and religious practices. Find common ground and seek solutions that allow both individuals to maintain their identities while also integrating aspects of each other's cultures and beliefs.

Flexibility and willingness to adapt can foster a stronger connection and understanding.

4. **Patience and Tolerance:** Building a relationship across cultural and religious boundaries requires patience and tolerance. Differences may lead to misunderstandings or conflicts at times, but approaching these challenges with an open heart and a willingness to learn can help overcome obstacles. Remember that it takes time to adjust and fully appreciate each other's unique perspectives.

5. **Family and Community Considerations:** When cultural and religious differences are significant, it is important to acknowledge the potential impact on your respective families and communities. Discuss how you will navigate potential challenges and how you can involve and educate your families about your relationship. Seeking their understanding and support can make a significant difference in building a harmonious bond.

6. **Celebrate Similarities and Differences:** Embrace the opportunity to explore and appreciate each other's cultures and traditions. Participate in cultural celebrations, religious ceremonies, or festivities together. This can deepen your connection, broaden your horizons, and foster a sense of unity.

7. **Seek Guidance and Support:** If you encounter significant challenges or find it challenging to navigate cultural or religious differences, consider seeking guidance from a counselor, religious leader, or cultural mentor. Their expertise and experience can provide valuable insights and assist you in finding constructive solutions.

Remember that cultural and religious differences can enrich a relationship by offering new perspectives, experiences, and opportunities for personal growth. By approaching these differences with respect, open communication, and a willingness to learn, you can build a strong and resilient bond that celebrates diversity and strengthens your connection.

Judged from past experiences
As you've experienced more relationships, it's natural to feel apprehensive about how your past experiences might influence your future love life. The fear of being judged based on previous relationships can be challenging to navigate, but it's important to remember that each new relationship is unique and should be approached with an open mind.

It's essential to acknowledge that everyone has a history, and it's natural to carry some emotional baggage from past relationships. However, it's crucial not to let those experiences define your future connections. Each person you encounter is an individual with their own perspectives, values, and understanding of relationships.

Here are a few things to keep in mind as you embark on new romantic endeavors:

1. **Embrace personal growth:** Every relationship, regardless of its outcome, provides an opportunity for personal growth and self-discovery. Reflect on your past experiences, identify the lessons you've learned, and work on becoming the best version of yourself. This growth will not only benefit you but also contribute to healthier and more fulfilling future relationships.

2. **Communicate openly:** Effective communication is key to building strong relationships. When you feel ready to explore a new connection, it's important to have open and honest conversations with your partner about your past experiences. Sharing your insights and concerns can foster understanding and create a foundation of trust.

3. **Avoid comparing:** Comparing your current partner to your previous ones can be detrimental to the relationship. Each

person is unique, and it's unfair to hold someone accountable for the actions or qualities of others. Try to approach each new relationship with fresh eyes and an open heart, allowing the person in front of you to reveal their own qualities and strengths.

4. **Set boundaries:** While it's important to be open and vulnerable, it's equally crucial to establish boundaries for yourself. Be clear about your needs, expectations, and what you're comfortable discussing regarding your past experiences. Healthy boundaries will help create a safe space for both you and your partner to grow together.

5. **Learn from the past without dwelling on it:** While it's natural to be influenced by past experiences, dwelling on them excessively can hinder the potential for a new connection to thrive. Instead, focus on the positive aspects and the lessons you've learned. Use that knowledge to make better choices, but also embrace the present moment and give yourself the chance to experience something new and different.

Remember, every relationship is an opportunity for growth, love, and connection. By being aware of your own emotions and fears and maintaining open communication with your partner, you can create a foundation of trust and understanding that will help you navigate any judgments from past experiences.

Your children - Other people's kids
Here comes a clever headline, there is a reason why that phrase came about, just like all other phrases and sayings. When you are a little older, the chance that your potential partner has children is very high. I really want to raise the issue of child rearing. If this wasn't on your list, it should be. If you don't have the same view on how children should be brought up, it will be almost completely impossible.

Difficulties with other children in a relationship can present unique challenges and require careful navigation. When entering a relationship with someone who already has children from a previous partnership or marriage, it's important to recognize that the dynamics and interactions involving the children can significantly impact the overall dynamics of the relationship. Here are some common difficulties that may arise:

1. **Parental loyalty and divided attention:** The parent in the relationship may feel torn between their new partner and their children. Balancing the needs of their partner and their children can be challenging, and it may cause tension and feelings of neglect on both sides.

2. **Establishing boundaries and discipline:** When two people come together with different parenting styles, it can be difficult to find a common ground. The new partner may have different expectations or approaches when it comes to discipline, rules, and routines. This can lead to conflicts and confusion for the children, as well as disagreements between the adults.

3. **Jealousy and rivalry:** Existing children may experience jealousy or rivalry towards the new partner, especially if they perceive them as a threat to their parent's attention or love. This can manifest in behavioral issues, acting out, or even attempts to sabotage the relationship.

4. **Blended family dynamics:** Blending two families together requires adjusting to new family roles and hierarchies. Children may struggle with accepting a new parental figure or sharing their parent's attention and resources with step-siblings. It takes time and effort to build trust, establish new routines, and foster a sense of unity among all family members.

5. **Co-parenting conflicts:** If the children have another parent who is involved in their lives, conflicts between the adults

may arise. Differences in parenting styles, communication breakdowns, or unresolved issues from the past can create tensions that affect the entire family.

6. **Emotional baggage and past trauma:** Children may carry emotional baggage or unresolved trauma from previous relationships or family disruptions. These experiences can impact their behavior, attachment patterns, and ability to form healthy relationships within the new family unit.

To address these difficulties, open and honest communication is vital. All parties involved need to express their feelings, concerns, and expectations while actively listening to each other's perspectives. Patience, empathy, and a willingness to compromise are crucial for building a harmonious and supportive environment for everyone. Seeking professional help, such as family therapy, can also provide valuable guidance and support in navigating these challenges. With time, effort, and a commitment to understanding, it is possible to overcome difficulties and foster a loving, blended family.

I have a friend who has entered a new marriage where his partner has a son who presents some challenges, he seems to be coping just fine and I asked him what his secret is? He told me that he simply doesn't care about each other's children. I Never enters into ""their" discussions, I always try to stay out. For myself, I realize that I don't really have that gift. In my world, that must require an iron psyche. Wish I had that! I always have a very strong need to express my point of view, it has almost never been successful.

That love from the beginning does not see the difficulties in this is completely understandable, but for example being in a relationship where you think there should be order and order, it is us parents who decide and the children show respect and find themselves in being children, where your partner appears to think that the children are equals. The children must be involved in all decisions, and each have a voice, when it is time to go to bed the children must know for themselves if it is time for them to sleep and so on, you understand what I mean, I hope. This is not going to be good, try to get this point on your list, it's my opinion is that it is hopeless not to have the same vision to make the family work, and through it make your relationship work. If the children are small, it will be very difficult to wait until they are old enough to move, no matter how much you love your partner. If there are only a few years left until the children move out, you can perhaps persevere, despite different views.

This may sound completely crazy what I'm talking about, but I think it's a very important point. Especially if there is an age difference between you and your partner. A few years can do a lot. Younger parents tend to want to interfere and let the children be involved in many decisions and dislike setting boundaries and having rules, I don't know why. It seems that the most important thing is to be "friends" with your children. Are you then the older partner in the relationship and come from more "old school" rules, i.e. that we have a responsibility as parents to prepare the children for adulthood and many times make decisions that they may not be happy about. Is that the case? Then I would say this can almost be a showstopper.

CHAPTER 9

INTIMACY AND SEXUALITY

CHAPTER 9 – Intimacy and Sexuality

Exploring physical intimacy at your own pace

Exploring physical intimacy when dating can be an exciting and meaningful part of building a romantic relationship. It's important to remember that physical intimacy should always be consensual and mutually desired by both partners. Everyone has their own comfort level and boundaries, so it's crucial to respect and communicate with each other to ensure a positive and enjoyable experience.

One of the keys to exploring physical intimacy at your own pace is open and honest communication. Discussing your expectations, desires, and boundaries with your partner can help create a safe and respectful environment. It's important to express your needs and listen to your partner's feelings and boundaries as well. This way, both of you can feel comfortable and secure as you navigate physical intimacy together.

Taking things slow allows both partners to gradually build trust and emotional connection. It gives you the opportunity to explore and understand each other's physical boundaries and preferences. By progressing at a pace that feels right for both of you, you can enjoy the journey of discovering each other's bodies and finding what brings pleasure and satisfaction to both parties.

It's also essential to be mindful of consent throughout the process. Consent is an ongoing, enthusiastic agreement between both individuals to engage in specific acts of physical intimacy. It should never be assumed or coerced. Checking in with each other, asking for verbal or non-verbal cues, and respecting any boundaries or signals is crucial to maintaining a healthy and enjoyable experience for both partners.

Remember that physical intimacy is not solely about sexual acts; it also includes other forms of affection and closeness, such as cuddling, holding hands, or simply spending quality time together.

Building emotional intimacy is equally important and can enhance the physical aspect of your relationship.

Exploring physical intimacy at your own pace allows you to prioritize your comfort and emotional well-being. It's perfectly acceptable to set boundaries and limits based on your personal values, beliefs, and comfort level. If at any point you feel unsure or uncomfortable, it's crucial to communicate openly with your partner and take the necessary steps to address any concerns or issues.

Dating is a journey of getting to know another person, and physical intimacy is just one aspect of that journey. Taking your time can foster a deeper connection and understanding between both partners, leading to a more fulfilling and intimate relationship. So, be patient, communicate openly, and enjoy the process of exploring physical intimacy in a way that feels right for you and your partner.

Communicating desires and consent
Communicating desires and consent when dating is an essential aspect of establishing healthy and respectful relationships. Open and honest communication is key to ensuring that both partners are on the same page and feel comfortable and secure in their interactions. By expressing desires and seeking consent, individuals can establish boundaries, build trust, and foster a strong foundation for their relationship.

When it comes to communicating desires, it's important to understand and acknowledge your own needs and wants. Reflecting on your values, boundaries, and personal preferences can help you gain clarity about what you are seeking in a relationship. This self-awareness enables you to effectively communicate your desires to your partner.

Effective communication of desires involves expressing yourself clearly and respectfully. Clearly articulating your wants and needs allows your partner to understand your expectations and consider them in the context of their own desires. Remember that open dialogue is a two-way street, and it's equally important to actively listen to your partner's desires and show empathy towards their needs.

Consent is a fundamental aspect of any healthy relationship. Consent means that all parties involved willingly agree to participate in a specific activity or engage in a certain level of intimacy. Consent should be given freely, without coercion, and can be withdrawn at any point. It is crucial to respect and honor each other's boundaries and to never assume that consent is implicit or permanent.

Obtaining consent involves ongoing communication and checking in with your partner. It's essential to create an environment where both partners feel comfortable expressing their boundaries and preferences. Respect your partner's decisions, and if they express discomfort or withdraw consent, it is crucial to honor their wishes without pressuring or guilting them.

Here are some tips for effectively communicating desires and consent when dating:

1. **Establish open lines of communication:** Encourage open and honest conversations from the beginning of the relationship. Create a safe space where both partners feel comfortable expressing their desires, concerns, and boundaries.

2. **Practice active listening:** Give your full attention to your partner when they are sharing their desires or concerns. Show empathy, ask clarifying questions, and validate their feelings.

3. **Use clear and respectful language:** Clearly express your desires, boundaries, and expectations using respectful and non-judgmental language. Avoid making assumptions about your partner's desires and actively seek their input.

4. **Check in regularly:** As the relationship progresses, continue to have regular conversations about desires, boundaries, and consent. People's preferences and comfort levels may change over time, so ongoing communication is crucial.

5. **Respect and honor boundaries:** Always respect your partner's boundaries and consent. Avoid pressuring or coercing them into activities they are not comfortable with and be prepared to adjust your own expectations if necessary.

6. **Be mindful of non-verbal cues:** Pay attention to non-verbal cues and body language. If your partner appears uncomfortable or hesitant, it's essential to pause and check in to ensure their continued consent.

7. **Educate yourself:** Take the initiative to educate yourself about consent, healthy relationships, and communication skills. Understanding the importance of consent and actively working on communication can greatly enhance your dating experience.

Remember, effective communication and consent are ongoing processes in any relationship. It requires effort, understanding, and respect from both partners. By prioritizing open dialogue and respecting each other's boundaries, you can create a dating experience that is grounded in mutual trust and understanding.

Maintaining a healthy sexual relationship
Maintaining a healthy sexual relationship is essential for overall well-being and the happiness of both partners involved. It requires open communication, mutual respect, and a willingness to explore and meet each other's needs. Here are some key factors to consider when seeking to maintain a healthy sexual relationship:

1. **Communication:** Open and honest communication is crucial when it comes to sexual intimacy. Discuss your desires, boundaries, and fantasies with your partner. Talk about what

feels good and what doesn't and be receptive to your partner's feedback as well. This will foster a deeper understanding of each other's needs and help build a stronger connection.

2. **Listening:** Listening is as important as expressing yourself. Pay attention to your partner's verbal and non-verbal cues. Be receptive to their needs, concerns, and desires. Creating a safe and non-judgmental space for your partner to share their thoughts and feelings will strengthen your emotional bond and enhance your sexual experiences.

3. **Mutual Respect:** Respect is the foundation of a healthy sexual relationship. Treat your partner with kindness, empathy, and consideration both inside and outside the bedroom. Respect their boundaries and never pressure or coerce them into any sexual activity. Consent should always be enthusiastic, ongoing, and given freely by both partners.

4. **Emotional Connection:** A strong emotional bond contributes significantly to sexual satisfaction. Take time to nurture your emotional connection by engaging in activities that strengthen your relationship, such as spending quality time together, expressing affection, and demonstrating love and support for one another.

5. **Variety and Exploration:** Sexual relationships benefit from variety and exploration. Experiment with different sexual activities, positions, and techniques. Be open to trying new things and discovering what brings pleasure to both you and your partner. This sense of exploration can reignite passion and prevent sexual routine from becoming monotonous.

6. **Prioritize Intimacy:** In a busy world, it's essential to prioritize intimacy. Make time for regular physical and emotional connection. Set aside moments for cuddling, kissing, and non-sexual intimacy. These acts foster intimacy and maintain a strong bond, even when life gets hectic.

7. **Sexual Health:** Maintain good sexual health practices by practicing safe sex, regularly getting tested for sexually transmitted infections (STIs) and discussing any concerns or symptoms with your partner. This not only ensures your well-being but also contributes to peace of mind, allowing you to fully enjoy your sexual relationship.

8. **Self-Care:** Taking care of yourself individually is vital for a healthy sexual relationship. Prioritize your physical and mental well-being, as they directly influence your sexual experiences. Exercise regularly, eat a balanced diet, manage stress, and address any personal issues or concerns that may affect your overall well-being.

Remember, each relationship is unique, and what works for one couple may not work for another. The key is to maintain open lines of communication, prioritize each other's needs, and approach the relationship with love, respect, and a spirit of exploration. By nurturing your sexual connection, you can create a fulfilling and healthy sexual relationship that brings joy and satisfaction to both partners involved.

CHAPTER 10

AGE GAP?

CHAPTER 10 – Age gap?

Whether or not you should date someone your own age is a personal decision that varies from person to person. There is no one-size-fits-all answer to this question as it depends on individual preferences, values, and compatibility.

Dating someone around your own age can have advantages such as shared life experiences, similar cultural references, and potentially easier compatibility when it comes to life goals and stages. Being in similar stages of life can make it easier to relate to each other and have common interests.

However, it's important to remember that age alone does not determine compatibility or the success of a relationship. Factors such as shared values, mutual respect, emotional connection, and overall compatibility play significant roles in the success of any relationship, regardless of age.

It is also worth noting that societal norms and expectations regarding age differences in relationships can vary. Some cultures or communities may have stricter expectations about dating within a certain age range, while others may be more open-minded.

Ultimately, the most important factor is that both individuals in the relationship are consenting adults and are happy and fulfilled in their partnership. It's essential to prioritize open communication, mutual respect, and a deep understanding of each other's needs and desires. By focusing on these aspects, you can make a decision that feels right for you and your potential partner, whether they are your age or not.

Speaking from personal experience, I have consistently been involved with younger women. This tendency of mine has become a running joke among my friends, who often tease me, saying, "You're always attracted to younger women." However, I beg to differ. My inclination towards younger women can be attributed to my rigorous weight training regimen, which I religiously follow for 5-6 days every week.

Additionally, I engage in 10 km walks on a daily basis. Consequently, despite being 60 years old, I possess a remarkable amount of energy. Therefore, I seek a partner who shares a similar level of vitality, a quality that is rarely found among individuals of my own age group.

If you meet someone not your age
When it comes to dating, the importance of an age gap depends on personal preferences and individual circumstances. While age can be a relevant factor in a relationship, it is not necessarily a definitive determinant of compatibility or success. Some people may prioritize age similarity, while others are more open to age differences.

Here are a few points to consider when it comes to age gaps in dating:

1. **Legal and ethical considerations:** It's important to ensure that the relationship is legal and consensual, as different jurisdictions have varying age of consent laws. Additionally, it's crucial to consider the power dynamics and potential imbalances that can arise in relationships with significant age gaps, particularly when one partner is significantly younger or less experienced.

2. **Life stages and goals:** Age can influence life experiences, goals, and priorities. Partners with significant age differences may be at different stages in their careers, personal growth, or desire for family and children. These factors can affect compatibility and long-term relationship prospects. It's essential to have open and honest discussions about life goals and expectations to assess compatibility.

3. **Emotional and intellectual compatibility:** Emotional and intellectual compatibility are significant determinants of relationship success. While age can influence these factors to some extent, they are not solely determined by age. Two individuals with a significant age difference can share

similar interests, values, and emotional maturity, leading to a fulfilling relationship.

4. **Social and cultural considerations:** Societal norms and cultural expectations surrounding age gaps can vary significantly. Some cultures or communities may frown upon relationships with substantial age differences, while others may be more accepting. It's important to be aware of these factors and consider how they might impact your relationship and the opinions of those around you.

Ultimately, the decision to care about an age gap in dating is subjective. It's crucial to consider factors such as legalities, life stages, emotional compatibility, and cultural context while respecting your own preferences and those of your potential partner. Open communication, mutual respect, and shared values are key to building a healthy and fulfilling relationship regardless of age differences.

CHAPTER 11

RED FLAGS AND WARNING SIGNS

CHAPTER 11 - Red Flags and Warning Signs

Identifying unhealthy patterns and toxic behaviors

When it comes to dating, it's essential to be aware of and identify unhealthy patterns and toxic behaviors. Recognizing these signs early on can help protect your emotional well-being and prevent potentially harmful relationships. Here are some key indicators to watch out for:

1. **Lack of respect:** Healthy relationships are built on mutual respect. If your partner consistently disrespects your boundaries, belittles your opinions, or disregards your feelings, it's a clear sign of a toxic behavior pattern.

2. **Control and manipulation:** A toxic partner often seeks to control and manipulate you. They may use guilt, intimidation, or emotional blackmail to get their way. Watch for signs of excessive jealousy, possessiveness, or attempts to isolate you from friends and family.

3. **Constant criticism:** Constructive feedback is normal in relationships, but a toxic partner will excessively criticize and demean you. They may undermine your self-esteem, making you feel unworthy or incompetent.

4. **Lack of accountability:** Healthy individuals take responsibility for their actions and apologize when they make mistakes. Toxic people tend to deflect blame onto others, making excuses or refusing to acknowledge their wrongdoings. They may also exhibit a pattern of repeat offenses without making genuine efforts to change.

5. **Emotional volatility:** Frequent mood swings, anger outbursts, or unpredictable behavior are red flags. If your partner's emotions are extreme and erratic, it can create an unstable and unsafe environment for you.

6. **Constant drama:** Toxic relationships are often characterized by an excessive amount of drama and chaos. If you find yourself constantly embroiled in arguments, conflicts, or situations that feel unnecessarily intense, it may be a sign of an unhealthy pattern.

7. **Gaslighting:** Gaslighting is a manipulative tactic used to make you doubt your own perceptions and sanity. A toxic partner may deny or twist the truth, making you question your memory, emotions, or experiences. They may invalidate your feelings or make you feel guilty for expressing them.

8. **Lack of support:** A healthy relationship involves supporting and encouraging each other's goals and aspirations. If your partner consistently undermines your dreams, lacks empathy, or fails to provide emotional support when you need it, it can be detrimental to your well-being.

9. **Boundary violations:** Respect for personal boundaries is crucial in any relationship. If your partner consistently ignores your boundaries, whether physical, emotional, or sexual, it's a significant sign of a toxic dynamic.

10. **Isolation from loved ones:** Toxic individuals may try to isolate you from your support system, including friends and family. They may discourage or prevent you from spending time with loved ones, making you solely reliant on them for emotional support and validation.

Remember, nobody is perfect, and occasional conflicts or disagreements are a normal part of any relationship. However, consistently encountering these unhealthy patterns and toxic behaviors is a clear indication that it's time to reassess the relationship and prioritize your own well-being. If you find yourself in such a situation, consider seeking support from trusted friends, family, or professionals who can help you navigate through it.

Trusting your instincts and seeking support

Trusting your instincts and seeking support when dating are two essential aspects of navigating the complex world of relationships. Dating can be an exciting but also challenging journey, filled with uncertainty and the potential for both joy and heartbreak. In such circumstances, it becomes crucial to rely on your instincts and intuition while also seeking support from trusted individuals. These two elements work hand in hand to help you make informed decisions and build meaningful connections.

Trusting your instincts means paying attention to your inner voice and the feelings that arise when you're interacting with someone you're interested in. Our instincts are often guided by subconscious cues and past experiences, helping us sense potential red flags or positive signs in a person or situation. When you trust your instincts, you give yourself the space to acknowledge and process these signals, allowing you to make choices that align with your values and well-being.

While trusting your instincts is important, it's equally vital to seek support from others when dating. Relationships are a complex interplay of emotions, expectations, and vulnerabilities, and discussing them with trusted friends, family members, or mentors can provide valuable perspectives and insights. Sharing your experiences and concerns with others who have your best interests at heart can help you gain new insights and consider different viewpoints. It can also offer emotional support, as you can lean on those around you during challenging times or when you need guidance.

Additionally, seeking support doesn't necessarily mean relying solely on friends and family. Professional relationship counselors or therapists can provide objective advice and help you navigate dating challenges with a more balanced perspective. These experts can assist you in understanding your own patterns and beliefs, as well as identifying areas for personal growth. Their expertise can be particularly valuable when dealing with complex emotions, past traumas, or insecurities that may impact your dating experiences.

When it comes to trusting your instincts and seeking support, it's important to strike a balance. While your instincts provide valuable guidance, it's essential to stay open-minded and consider different viewpoints. Seeking support helps broaden your understanding and offers an external perspective that can help validate or challenge your own instincts. By combining these two elements, you can make more informed decisions, navigate potential pitfalls, and build healthier, more fulfilling relationships.

In conclusion, trusting your instincts and seeking support are essential pillars in the realm of dating. By trusting your instincts, you honor your inner wisdom and use it as a compass to guide your choices. Simultaneously, seeking support from trusted individuals or professionals can provide you with valuable insights, emotional support, and objective advice. Together, these elements empower you to make informed decisions, protect your well-being, and foster meaningful connections in the world of dating.

CHAPTER 12

DATING FOR THE HAPPY AND PERMANENT RELATIONSHIP

CHAPTER 12 - Dating for the happy and permanent relationship

Navigating the transition from dating to a committed relationship

Navigating the transition from dating to a committed relationship can be an exciting and sometimes challenging process. It signifies a shift from casual dating to a more serious and exclusive partnership. If you find yourself wanting to take your relationship to the next level, here are some steps to help you navigate this transition successfully:

1. **Reflect on your own feelings:** Before initiating the transition, take some time to reflect on your own feelings and intentions. Consider why you want to move into a committed relationship and what it means to you. Assess your readiness for the commitment and make sure you genuinely care for your partner and see a future together.

2. **Communication is key:** Open and honest communication is crucial during this transition. Have a conversation with your partner about your desires and expectations. Share your feelings and intentions and ask for their input as well. It's important to be clear about what you both want and ensure you're on the same page.

3. **Assess the compatibility and long-term potential:** Evaluate the compatibility and long-term potential of your relationship. Consider your shared values, goals, and aspirations. Discuss important topics such as family, finances, career aspirations, and lifestyle choices. Assess whether you have similar visions for the future and if your relationship has the potential to grow and thrive in the long run.

4. **Spend quality time together:** During this transition, spend quality time together and engage in activities that strengthen your bond. Plan meaningful dates, explore shared hobbies, and create new experiences together. Building a solid

foundation of shared memories and positive experiences can help solidify your commitment to each other.

5. **Introduce each other to your social circles:** Introducing your partner to your friends and family signifies a deeper level of commitment. It demonstrates that you're serious about your relationship and want your loved ones to be a part of your lives. Similarly, be open to meeting and getting to know your partner's friends and family. Embrace these new connections as they can help foster a sense of belonging and integration.

6. **Establish boundaries and expectations:** As you transition into a committed relationship, it's essential to establish clear boundaries and expectations. Discuss topics like exclusivity, trust, communication, and commitment. Address any concerns or fears you may have and work together to find solutions that align with both of your needs.

7. **Allow for a natural progression:** Remember that transitioning from dating to a committed relationship is a process that takes time. It's important to allow the relationship to naturally progress and avoid rushing things. Let the connection grow organically and be patient with each other. Building a strong foundation takes time, and it's important to nurture the relationship along the way.

8. **Seek support when needed:** If you encounter difficulties or uncertainties during this transition, don't hesitate to seek support. Talk to a trusted friend, family member, or even a therapist who can provide guidance and insight. Having an outside perspective can be valuable in navigating challenges and ensuring a smooth transition.

Remember that every relationship is unique, and the transition from dating to a committed relationship will vary for each couple. The key is to maintain open communication, mutual respect, and a willingness to grow together. By taking these steps, you'll be better equipped to navigate this transition successfully and build a strong, fulfilling relationship.

Building a strong foundation for a lasting partnership
Building a strong foundation for a lasting partnership is crucial for creating a healthy, fulfilling, and successful relationship. Whether it's a romantic partnership, a business collaboration, or any other type of partnership, certain key principles and practices can help foster a strong foundation. Here are some essential steps to consider:

1. **Effective Communication:** I say it again, communication forms the backbone of any partnership. It's essential to establish open, honest, and respectful lines of communication from the very beginning. Encourage active listening, express your thoughts and feelings clearly, and be receptive to feedback. Regularly check in with each other to ensure you are on the same page and address any concerns or conflicts promptly.

2. **Trust and Transparency:** Trust is the bedrock of a lasting partnership. Cultivate trust by being transparent and honest with each other. Avoid keeping secrets or hiding information that might affect the partnership. Build trust through consistent reliability, follow-through on commitments, and maintaining confidentiality when required. Trust forms the basis for collaboration, innovation, and problem-solving.

3. **Shared Values and Goals:** Partnerships thrive when there is alignment in values and goals. It's essential to have discussions early on to understand each other's core values, vision, and aspirations. Identify common ground and shared objectives that can serve as a unifying force. When partners are working towards a common purpose, it strengthens the partnership and fosters a sense of shared ownership.

4. **Mutual Respect and Support:** Treat your partner with respect and dignity. Recognize and appreciate their

strengths, contributions, and individuality. Encourage each other's growth, celebrate successes, and provide support during challenging times. A foundation built on mutual respect creates an environment where partners feel valued and motivated to give their best.

5. **Conflict Resolution:** Conflicts and disagreements are inevitable in any partnership. It's essential to approach conflicts constructively, viewing them as opportunities for growth rather than as obstacles. Develop effective conflict resolution skills by practicing active listening, seeking to understand different perspectives, and finding mutually agreeable solutions. Respectful and fair resolution of conflicts strengthens the partnership in the long run.

6. **Collaboration and Flexibility:** Foster a spirit of collaboration and teamwork. Embrace the idea that you are working together to achieve shared goals. Encourage input from all partners, leverage each other's strengths, and promote a culture of shared decision-making. Remain flexible and adaptable as circumstances change, allowing the partnership to evolve and grow over time.

7. **Continuous Learning and Improvement:** A strong partnership requires a commitment to continuous learning and improvement. Be open to feedback, both giving and receiving it graciously. Encourage a culture of ongoing personal and professional development. Invest in regular evaluations to assess the partnership's progress, identify areas for improvement, and make necessary adjustments.

Remember, building a strong foundation for a lasting partnership is an ongoing process that requires effort, dedication, and commitment from all parties involved. By prioritizing effective communication, trust, respect.

Managing shared responsibilities and future planning

Managing shared responsibilities and future planning is essential for maintaining a successful and sustainable partnership. Whether it's a personal relationship, a business venture, or any other collaborative endeavor, having a clear framework for responsibilities and a shared vision for the future is crucial. Here are some key steps to effectively manage shared responsibilities and engage in future planning:

1. **Define Roles and Responsibilities:** Start by clearly defining the roles and responsibilities of each partner. Determine who is responsible for specific tasks, projects, or areas of expertise. This clarity helps prevent misunderstandings, avoids duplication of efforts, and ensures that everyone knows what is expected of them. Regularly revisit and update these roles as needed, especially when new projects or challenges arise.

2. **Open and Transparent Communication:** Maintain open and transparent communication when it comes to sharing responsibilities. Discuss expectations, preferences, and any concerns or challenges that may arise. Regularly communicate progress, updates, and changes in responsibilities to keep everyone informed and aligned. Encourage feedback and suggestions from all partners to foster a collaborative and inclusive environment.

3. **Establish Clear Goals and Objectives:** Set clear, measurable goals and objectives for the partnership. These should be aligned with the shared vision and values of all partners. Clearly define what success looks like and create a roadmap to achieve those goals. Break down larger objectives into smaller milestones to track progress and celebrate achievements along the way. Regularly evaluate and adjust goals as necessary to adapt to changing circumstances.

4. **Strategic Planning:** Engage in strategic planning to envision the future of the partnership. Assess the current landscape, identify opportunities and potential challenges, and develop

strategies to capitalize on strengths and mitigate risks. Create a shared vision for the future and outline specific steps to achieve it. Set timelines, allocate resources, and establish benchmarks to track progress. Regularly review and update the strategic plan as needed to ensure its relevance and effectiveness.

5. **Delegation and Collaboration:** Distribute responsibilities and tasks among partners based on their strengths, skills, and expertise. Delegate tasks that align with each partner's capabilities and interests. Foster a collaborative environment where partners work together, leveraging their collective knowledge and experience. Encourage open dialogue, brainstorming, and problem-solving sessions to generate innovative ideas and approaches.

6. **Flexibility and Adaptability:** Recognize that plans may change, and flexibility is necessary in managing shared responsibilities and future planning. Be open to adjustments and refinements along the way. Embrace a mindset of learning from both successes and failures, allowing the partnership to evolve and grow. Stay informed about industry trends, market conditions, and external factors that may influence the partnership's direction.

7. **Regular Evaluation and Course Correction:** Schedule regular evaluations to assess the partnership's progress, effectiveness, and alignment with goals. Reflect on achievements, challenges, and areas for improvement. Solicit feedback from all partners and use it to identify areas that require course correction or additional support. Regularly revisit the strategic plan, making necessary adjustments to ensure continued growth and success.

By actively managing shared responsibilities and engaging in future planning, partners can work together more effectively, maximize their collective potential, and build a solid foundation for long-term success.

Can you do too much dating?

Dating multiple people simultaneously, often referred to as "dating too many," is a personal choice that varies depending on individual preferences, circumstances, and cultural norms. While there is no universal consensus on whether it is acceptable or advisable, it's essential to consider the potential benefits and challenges associated with dating multiple people at once.

One potential advantage of dating multiple individuals is the opportunity to explore different connections and understand personal preferences better. It allows individuals to gain a broader perspective on what they value in a partner, experience different dynamics, and learn more about themselves in the process. This approach can help individuals make informed decisions about their romantic interests and potentially lead to finding a compatible long-term partner.

However, it's important to navigate multiple dating scenarios with honesty, integrity, and open communication. It is crucial to ensure that all parties involved are aware of the situation and consent to the non-exclusive nature of the relationships. Maintaining transparency and managing expectations is essential to prevent misunderstandings, hurt feelings, or unintended consequences.

Dating multiple people can also present challenges. It requires effective time management and emotional energy to balance the demands of multiple relationships simultaneously. It's crucial to ensure that no one feels neglected or becomes a secondary priority in the process. Communication skills and emotional intelligence play a significant role in navigating such situations successfully.

Additionally, dating multiple people might involve complexities in terms of emotional attachment and commitment. Developing strong emotional connections with multiple individuals simultaneously can be demanding and may require careful emotional navigation to avoid hurt feelings or confusion.

Furthermore, cultural and societal norms may influence the acceptability of dating multiple people at once. In some cultures or communities, it might be frowned upon or considered inappropriate. It is essential to be aware of and respect the prevailing norms and values in one's social context.

Ultimately, the decision to date multiple people or focus on one individual should be based on personal values, comfort levels, and what feels right for each person. It's crucial to be mindful of the emotional well-being of oneself and others involved in order to maintain healthy and respectful relationships.

Remember that open communication, honesty, and empathy are key components of successful dating, regardless of whether you choose to date one person or multiple individuals.

Dating can be an exciting and fulfilling experience, allowing individuals to explore romantic connections and develop meaningful relationships. However, like any aspect of life, excessive dating can have an impact on one's emotions. While dating too much in itself may not be inherently negative, the intensity, frequency, and emotional investment in multiple relationships can affect a person's emotional well-being in several ways.

1. **Emotional Exhaustion:** Dating requires time, effort, and emotional energy. When someone constantly engages in dating activities without taking breaks to recharge, they may experience emotional exhaustion. Juggling multiple dates, conversations, and expectations can be overwhelming, leaving individuals feeling drained and emotionally depleted. This can lead to increased stress, irritability, and a lack of enthusiasm in future dating endeavors.

2. **Disappointment and Rejection:** Engaging in numerous dates can increase the likelihood of encountering disappointment and rejection. Not every dating experience will result in a lasting connection, and repeated experiences of rejection

can take a toll on one's self-esteem and emotional state. Constantly investing emotions in multiple people and facing rejection from some can lead to feelings of inadequacy, sadness, and frustration.

3. **Conflicting Emotions:** When dating multiple people simultaneously, individuals may find themselves experiencing conflicting emotions. They might feel torn between different partners or uncertain about their own feelings. This internal conflict can generate anxiety, guilt, and confusion, making it challenging to make decisions or establish genuine emotional connections.

4. **Shallow Emotional Connections:** Dating too much may hinder the development of deep emotional connections. When individuals are constantly meeting new people and going on dates without allowing sufficient time for meaningful interaction and understanding, relationships may remain superficial. This can result in a lack of emotional intimacy and a sense of emptiness or dissatisfaction.

5. **Emotional Comparisons:** Engaging in multiple dating experiences can lead to constant comparisons between partners. This can create feelings of insecurity, jealousy, and self-doubt. Continually evaluating one's connections and questioning if they measure up to others can have a detrimental effect on self-esteem and overall emotional well-being.

6. **Emotional Burnout:** Over time, excessive dating can lead to emotional burnout. The constant cycle of meeting new people, going on dates, and experiencing emotional highs and lows can become draining. Emotional burnout can manifest as apathy, detachment, or a decreased desire to continue dating altogether.

It is important to note that the impact of dating on emotions can vary greatly depending on individual circumstances, personal resilience, and how one approaches dating. Some individuals may thrive in the dating scene, while others may find it overwhelming. It is crucial to prioritize self-care, establish healthy boundaries, and take breaks when needed to ensure emotional well-being while dating.

CHAPTER 13

EMBRACING THE JOURNEY

CHAPTER 13 - Embracing the Journey

As you reach the final chapter of "THE LIST: A Modern Guide to Dating, it's time to reflect on your journey thus far and embrace the experiences that have shaped you. Dating and relationships are not just about finding the perfect partner; they are about personal growth, self-discovery, and embracing the unknown.

Throughout this book, you have explored various aspects of dating, from understanding yourself and what you want, to navigating the world of online dating and building healthy relationships. You have learned the art of communication, mastered the first date, and discovered the importance of trust, respect, and setting boundaries.

Now, as you move forward, it's essential to remember that the journey doesn't end here. Dating and relationships are dynamic and ever evolving, and it's crucial to continue learning and growing along the way.

1. **Your list:** Establish the requirements for your future partner, ensuring a minimum of 10 distinct aspects. Let you list go from your most important priorities to priorities you can live with.

2. **Determine which criteria from your list are truly crucial and their level of importance:** Are there showstoppers that you cannot compromise on? If so, it's essential to acknowledge these priorities before allowing yourself to develop deep feelings. If such deal-breakers exist, no matter how comprehensive your checklist may be, they won't hold much significance because your emotions will override it.

3. **Embrace Personal Development:** Remember that the purpose of dating extends beyond finding a companion; it is also an opportunity for self-discovery. Embrace personal growth by continually exploring your values, passions, and goals. Dedicate time to nurturing your own happiness and well-being, independent of any romantic relationship.

4. **Maintain Openness:** Stay open-minded and open-hearted as you encounter new people and experiences. Approach each interaction as an opportunity to learn, grow, and connect with others. Remember that everyone has their own unique story and perspective to share.

5. **Embrace Imperfections:** Understand that perfection does not exist in relationships. Embrace the imperfections and challenges that come your way. Relationships require effort, compromise, and understanding. It's the willingness to work through difficulties that strengthens the bond between two individuals.

6. **Prioritize Communication:** Effective communication is the cornerstone of any healthy relationship. Continue developing your communication skills, both in expressing your needs and actively listening to your partner. Be open, honest, and compassionate in your conversations.

7. **Embrace Vulnerability:** True intimacy requires vulnerability. Allow yourself to be seen, heard, and understood by your partner. Share your fears, dreams, and insecurities, knowing that true connection stems from being authentically yourself.

8. **Learn from Challenges:** Challenges are inevitable in relationships. Instead of viewing them as roadblocks, see them as opportunities for growth. Learn from past experiences, seek support when needed, and use these challenges as stepping stones towards a stronger and healthier relationship.

9. **Embrace Adventure:** Relationships should be a journey filled with adventure, exploration, and shared experiences. Embrace new adventures together, whether it's traveling to new places, trying new hobbies, or simply exploring new facets of each other's personalities.

10. **Celebrate Each Other:** Remember to celebrate your partner's accomplishments and milestones. Be their biggest supporter and cheerleader, and encourage them to pursue their passions and dreams. Celebrate the small victories in your relationship and express gratitude for each other's presence in your lives.

As you wrap up your journey through "THE LIST: A Modern Guide to Dating and keep in mind that discovering love and cultivating a satisfying partnership is not a fixed endpoint but an ever-evolving expedition. Embrace the wisdom you have acquired, remain authentic to your core values, and approach every new phase with receptiveness and open-mindedness.

This book is one you can revisit time and time again, for within its pages lie the fundamental principles: honesty, authenticity, active listening, effective communication, trust, transparency, patience, tolerance. Why do I reiterate these points? Because they cannot be stressed enough. The significance of these principles defies explanation.

Above all, remember that the most important relationship you will ever have is the one you have with yourself. Love and respect yourself, try to be the best version of yourself and the rest will fall into place. Happy dating and may your journey be filled with love, growth, and lasting happiness!

Wish you all the best
Kennet Bath

Printed in the United States
by Baker & Taylor Publisher Services